IAN HAMBLETON.

REGULATING HEALTH
AND SAFETY AT WORK:
THE WAY FORWARD

REGULATING HEALTH AND SAFETY AT WORK: THE WAY FORWARD

**EDITED BY PROFESSOR PHIL JAMES
AND DR DAVID WALTERS**

THE INSTITUTE OF EMPLOYMENT RIGHTS

Institute of Employment Rights
177 Abbeville Road, London SW4 9RL

020 7498 6919, fax 020 498 9080
ier@gn.apc.org, www.ier.org.uk

First published 1999

ISBN 1 873271 72 7

British Library Cataloguing in Publication data
A catalogue record for this book is available from the British Library

Designed and typeset by the Institute of Employment Rights
Printed by Redwood Books, Trowbridge

Contents

Acknowledgements

THIS report could not have been prepared without the efforts of the more than thirty trade unionists, academics and lawyers who gave up their time to participate in the project's working groups and in particular, the chairs of those groups – David Bergman, Simon Pickvance, David Walters and Charles Woolfson.

Its content has also benefited from those who agreed to give evidence before the public committees of enquiry which were held as part of the project.

Finally, the project would not have been completed without the sterling support provided by Carolyn Jones, the Institute's Director, and the efficient work carried out by Megan Dobney on the book's production.

Professor Phil James

Foreword

THERE is nothing more important than maintaining the health and safety of people at work. Yet each year there are around 1.6 million people injured at work. At the same time, around 2 million people suffer illness that is directly caused or made worse by their employment.

With the enactment of the Health and Safety at Work Act 1974, the legal base for a new approach to health and safety was established. Based on principles set out in the Robens Report published in 1972, the Act initiated a change that has improved health and safety standards within the workplace. Coupled with the introduction of trade union Safety Representatives in 1978, the 1974 Act still provides a good base from which to move into a new century.

Since the Robens Committee produced its report, major changes have taken place within the economy. The large corporate manufacturing companies with tens of thousands of employees have given way to smaller organisations. Employment relationships have changed. Today we see a decline in labour intensive heavy industry; a growth in service activities; contracting out of the support activities of organisations, while they concentrate on their 'core activities'; the casualisation of the workforce; increasing employment of women, older and disabled workers – as rehabilitation pressures apply; and a large growth in small businesses.

Health and safety at work cannot be viewed in isolation. The quality of employment, environmental changes, competitive pressures, globalisation, and new technologies, are all contributing to major changes at work. We are in a period of rapid change. Many of these could not have been foreseen by the Robens Committee. Yet they need to be addressed. The Institute's report *Robens Revisited* provided analysis of such issues and looked forward in seeking solutions.

It is timely then, that the Institute of Employment Rights now publish their new report, *Regulating Health & Safety at Work: the way forward*. In a unique exercise, the IER has brought together some of the leading health and safety specialists in the UK. By establishing specialist groups and holding Committees of Enquiry, theories have been tested and views of a wide audience sought. The result is an authoritative report which reflects on the key aims of the Robens Committee. Whilst looking back at the success and failures of the last 25 years, those involved with this project have put forward many thought provoking views on what we need to do in the next 25 years.

It is expected that this report will influence the current thinking on health and safety at work. The government has already launched their *Revitalising Health and Safety* initiative, to mark the 25th Anniversary of the Health and Safety at Work Act 1974. During 1999, the Health and Safety Commission will launch their Discussion Document on effective workforce involvement in raising health and safety standards. *Regulating Health & Safety at Work: the way forward* will undoubtedly help shape the thinking around these initiatives.

Out of all the issues addressed, it is the involvement of the workforce which is a vital component of future action in the health and safety field. Trade unions have demonstrated that they have had a major influence on improving health and safety standards. Yet the role of the safety representatives is still downplayed. In reality, the Robens Committee principle of 'self regulation' can only be effective if the workforce have an opportunity for 'balanced participation'. This is best achieved by employers and safety representatives working together to resolve health and safety problems.

As we approach a new year, a new century and a new millennium, there are many challenges that face people at work. Those working on this project; those who have commented upon the drafts; those who have given their time freely to thinking about all the issues are to be congratulated. *Regulating Health & Safety at Work: the way forward* is an excellent review of workplace health and safety. I would commend it to anyone who is interested in improving health and safety standards at work. In time, I expect it to become a key reference book for anybody seriously interested in preventing occupational accidents and ill-health.

Work should enhance life, it should not endanger it. This report provides a review of what needs to be done to prevent accidents and ill-health in the workplace.

John Edmonds
General Secretary GMB

Introduction

THIS book represents the outcome of a project organised by the Institute of Employment Rights in order to examine the present regulation of health and safety in Britain under the Health and Safety at Work (HSW) Act with a view to:

- identifying areas of weakness in the present system of regulation; and
- making recommendations aimed at:
  — strengthening the protection of people from work-related risks;
  — improving the position of workers harmed as a result of such risks; and
  — enhancing the economic incentives and benefits associated with promoting and maintaining a safe and healthier work environment.

The HSW Act was placed on the statute book twenty-five years ago. It was an Act which, in a number of significant ways, introduced a departure from previous approaches to regulating health and safety. There is no doubt that this new approach had an impact on the way in which health and safety was regulated and especially on the involvement of employers and trade unions in the process. It also probably contributed to the raising of the profile of health and safety issues in the public consciousness. However, the period since its introduction has seen dramatic changes occur in the environment within which health and safety is regulated. These changes inevitably raise fundamental questions about the continued relevance of the statutory system put in place by the Act.

Many of these questions, and the challenges posed by them, were identified and discussed in an earlier interim report on the project[1]. In the pages that follow we move on to examine these challenges in more detail and consider what steps should be taken in response to them in order to further the above objectives. The proposals for reform put forward are, in our view, based on a realistic analysis of the problems of regulating health and safety in the current environment and constitute a firm basis for creating a safer and healthier environment for both people at work and those affected by work activities. We also believe that they will make an important contribution to current debates about the regulation of workplace health and safety – debates which have been given added relevance and poignancy by two recent developments. First, the publication earlier this year by the Health and Safety Commission (HSC) and the Department for the Environment, Transport and the Regions (DETR) of a consultative document on the future of health and safety regulation[2]. Secondly, the appalling rail disaster at Paddington.

Why a review of health and safety is needed

ALTHOUGH the HSW Act undoubtedly represented a significant milestone in the regulation of health and safety in Britain, we are less certain of the unqualified success that is often claimed for it. In particular, we think that there are a number of reasons why it is both important and opportune to review the experience of health and safety regulation under the Act. They include the following.

The continuing toll of work-related harm

The scale of harm that both workers and the public experience as a result of work activity continues to be of enormous magnitude. The relevant figures are well known and will be referred to in some details in the subsequent chapters. In brief, however, they indicate that thousands of workers and former workers die each year as a result of work-related injuries and ill health. They also suggest that over a million employees, representing around 4% of the workforce, suffer a work-related injury each year; that more than two million people, or around 5% of the population of workers and ex-workers, suffer from an illness which they believe was caused or made worse by their work; and that in excess of 25,000 workers who have been injured or made ill by work leave the workforce each year.

The scale of this harm is clearly disturbing, to say the least. However, the picture becomes even more worrying when account is taken of the impact of work activity on members of the public. Readers will of course already be well aware of the major disasters brought about by failings of safety systems in public services such as at Kings' Cross, Zeebrugge, Clapham Junction and most recently, Paddington. They may well be less aware of the fact that incidents involving the public account for nearly one third of reported work-related accident fatalities.

This harm clearly imposes untold pain and suffering on its victims and their families. It also imposes enormous costs on employers, via such sources as working days lost, sick pay provision, insurance premiunms, and lost production, and the taxpayer, through social security payments and medical treatment provided by the National Health Service. Yet, despite this, the health and safety establishment still tends to regard the HSW Act as a great success.

It seems to us that such a conclusion is based on rather dubious evidence. While it is true that there has been a decline in the number of recorded fatalities and serious injuries resulting from work-related incidents, this is not solely due to the operation of the 1974 Act, since shifts in the structure of employment and technological developments have also played an important role. Indeed, the Health and Safety Executive (HSE) itself acknowledges that at least one third of the fall in fatalities over the past twenty-five years is the result of changes in the pattern of employment. In addition, and more generally, it also admits that during the 1990s the fatal injury rate for employees has effectively reached a plateau.

Questionable appropriateness of the statutory framework

The HSW Act was based on the 1972 recommendations of the Committee of Inquiry on Safety and Health at Work – the Robens Committee. The Robens report was prepared at a time when a large proportion of work activity was undertaken by male, full-time employees working for large, unionised companies in the manufacturing and extractive industries. Subsequently, the world of work has changed dramatically. For example, employment in the services sector and small and medium-sized enterprises has become far more important, trade union membership and recognition has fallen significantly, and there has been a marked growth of "non-standard" forms of employment, such as self-employment and part-time and temporary working. There seem no grounds for assuming that an approach to regulation conceived at the time of Robens continues to be either relevant or appropriate. Or, as the HSC and government argue, that the HSW Act has stood the test of time. Indeed, the Robens Committee itself observed that:

"There are no good reasons for merely assuming that our traditional approach to the control of these problems necessarily corresponds to what is really needed today or what maybe is needed in the future."[3]

However, it is not just the changes in the structure of employment that have occurred over the last twenty-five years that raise questions about the appropriateness of the HSW Act. For this period has also seen cuts in the welfare state, changes to the system of personal injury litigation and a growing awareness of the inadequate provision made for the treatment of ill and injured workers. In combination these issues have served to draw attention to the need to both explore the current arrangements in place in respect of both the compensation and rehabilitation of workers harmed by their work and to consider whether closer links should be established between these arrangements and the legal framework in place to prevent work-related harm.

Growth of public concern

Another aspect of change that has become evident since the introduction of the HSW Act is the shifts that have taken place in societal expectations and public perceptions and awareness concerning the relationship between work and worker and public well-being. These shifts have been demonstrated in a number of ways. For example, during the last two decades there has been:

- a growing intolerance of risk on the part of the public;
- a shift from concern about worker health and safety per se to a wider concern about the impact of business activity on the public;
- a growth in scientific and popular literature dealing with risk and risk communication;
- greater media attention to health and safety issues, such as the control of asbestos, occupational asthma, work-related upper limb disorders, and the psychosocial effects of the intensification of work;
- an increased readiness to press for retribution and compensation where harm has been caused by work activities;
- widespread media and public interest in the development of corporate manslaughter law, particularly in the aftermath of work-related incidents in which members of the public have died;
- increased public expectations of access to information, along with associated demands for greater transparency and accountability; and
- a greater demand for public involvement in decision-making processes that have implications for public safety.

These changes in societal expectations and perceptions may have partly stemmed from the participative decision-making processes utilised by both the HSC and HSE. However, they also seem to reflect more general forces. For example, changes in attitudes to the nature and acceptability of work-related risks; a growing concern with environmental risks, which sociologists argue is symptomatic of a society in which the social production of wealth is systematically accompanied by the social production of risk[4]; and societal resistance to the global economic, social, personal and cultural changes that are occurring as a result of the massive impact of new technology in the post-industrial society[5]. Whatever there causes, however, they undoubtedly represent a major challenge to the existing system for the regulation of work-related risks which requires a response from government and health and safety regulators.

The renewal of social democracy

For most of the time that the HSW Act has been in force the country was governed by a succession of Conservative governments whose political agendas were fundamentally different to the one in place at the time it was passed. These governments systematically dismantled the corporatist state which had underpinned the tripartitism of the Act, made successive attempts to deregulate health and safety, and generally did as little as possible to implement new European health and safety requirements. Overall, this approach did nothing to improve health and safety standards and arguably, lowered them.

The election of a Labour government in 1997 brought with it the possibility to reverse the direction of this drift and develop a revitalised strategy on health and safety at work. The recent DETR/HSC consultation exercise on the future of health and safety regulation demonstrates the potential for the development of such a new strategy. However, practical action to date has been limited – apart from some restoration of HSE funding, legislation to protect whistleblowers and the promise of measures on corporate manslaughter. At the same time the wider canvas of the present government's policy agenda has potentially important implications for the regulation of occupational health and safety.

In a series of white papers, such as those on improving competitiveness through the development of a knowledge-based economy[6], modernising government[7], sustainable development[8] and public health[9], the government has utilised a new lexicon which is replete with references to forging "new partnerships", engaging and involving "stakeholders" and undertaking more "joined-up" working across government departments. This same language features prominently in the HSC's strategic plan for the next three years[10] and the joint statement that it and the Department of Health issued covering occupational and public health[11]. It is also prominent in the recent DETR/HSC consultative document.

This language can be seen to reflect a desire on the part of the government to create a political economy in which a renewal of social democracy can occur at the same time as a revitalised and globally competitive economy is created[12]. It can also be seen to echo similar developments in many other countries of the European Union and the strategies which are being developed to underpin "Social Europe" within the Union. For example, those under discussion in relation to the notion of "employability".

What is exciting about these developments is that they offer the possibility of viewing the governance and regulation of health and safety as forming a central element in both the re-defining of social democracy and the establishment of a more competitive economy. As a result, perhaps uniquely in its history, the issue of workplace health and safety has the potential to emerge from its traditional peripheral role in society and the economy and join issues which occupy the central stage of social and economic policy development. In doing so the opportunity opens up to conceptualise health and safety in far broader terms and in particular, to see it as extending to encompass not just the prevention of work-related harm, but the more productive design of work, the treatment of illness and injury and the provision of compensation to those who are unable to work as a result of such harm.

The use of a new political lexicon does not, however, mean that this potential will be realised. Rather its realisation will require a willingness on the part of the government, and the European Union, to be prepared to consider the making of radical changes to the way in which health and safety is regulated, if, as we believe, the existing system cannot be adequately improved by relatively minor reforms. Otherwise a valuable opportunity will have been missed to put in place a system of regulation that can indeed ensure that workers are able to productively go about their work activities without incurring injury and ill health.

The focus and structure of the project

THE project has been constructed around several themes which between them include a consideration of the following issues:

- the extent of change in the environment of health and safety regulation over the past 25 years;
- the consequences of this change for the nature of work-related harm and its regulation;
- the governance of accountability for personal injury, ill health or death, as well as other related loss or damage;
- the processes by which the risks to workers and others who may be affected by work activities are assessed and managed by employers and other duty holders;
- the role played by workers' representatives in the development

and operation of these processes; and

- the means for treating, compensating and rehabilitating workers harmed by their work.

In adopting a thematic approach, an over-arching aim of the project was not only to develop the themes themselves, but to explore the extent of their inter-connections and the further connections that exist between them and the wider economy, including the organisation of business and the social welfare system in place. It is hoped that the result of this approach is the provision of a more holistic review of the system for regulating and ameliorating the risks to health and safety than is usually attempted. At the same time the review does not claim to be entirely comprehensive. A project of this scale, undertaken without the benefit of research funds or government sponsorship, has, of necessity, to be selective. We are conscious, for example, that the review does not explore fully the relationship between health and safety regulation and the protection of the environment. We are also aware that our treatment of the HSW Act does not provide a detailed analysis of the operation of the duties placed on manufacturers and suppliers. These are important areas and there is much more to be said about them. However, we hope that we have said enough in the following pages to stimulate further discussion of these issues.

The book has been structured in a manner which largely reflects the way in which the Institute's project was developed. We have already referred to the interim report for the project in which the need for a review of health and safety regulation was discussed. Following its publication in 1998, the project steering group set about organising separate working groups covering the themes identified. The groups drew extensively on the experience and expertise of their membership and in addition held a number of special public committees of enquiry to pursue some of the emerging issues. Reports from the working groups form the basis of the chapters on employers and their statutory duties (chapter 2), the administration of the statutory framework (chapter 3), worker representation (chapter 4) and the amelioration of work-related harm (chapter 5). These chapters are preceeded by a scene-setting chapter which outlines the existing statutory framework and discusses the key factors which have influenced its development since 1974.

Chapters 2-5 each provide a discussion of the structure and operation of the present system as it relates to the particular theme with which they are concerned. They all also identify weaknesses in the current arrangements discussed and put forward a series of specific recommendations that we believe will contribute to the establishment of an improved system for occupational health and safety which more adequately prevents work-related harm and ameliorates its consequences. The final chapter draws these recommendations together and also details our overall conclusions concerning the adequacy of the present system.

Notes

1 D. Walters and P. James, *Robens Revisited: The Case for a Review of Occupational Health and Safety Legislation*, 1998, Institute of Employment Rights.
2 Department for the Environment, Transport and the Regions/Health and Safety Commission, *Revitalising Health and Safety, Consultation Document*, 1999, DETR.
3 Lord Robens, *Safety and Health at Work: Report of the Committee 1970-1972*, Cmnd 5034, HMSO.
4 U. Beck, *Risk Society*, 1992, Sage.
5 M. Castells, *The Information Age: Economy, Society and Culture*, 1998, Blackwell.
6 Department of Trade and Industry, *Building the Knowledge Driven Economy*, 1999, Stationary Office.
7 Cabinet Office, *Modernising Government*, 1999, Stationary Office.
8 Department for the Environment, Transport and the Regions, *A Better Quality of Life: A Strategy for Sustainable Development in the United Kingdom*, 1999, Stationary Office.
9 Department of Health, *Our Healthier Nation: A Contract for Health*, Cmnd 3852, 1998, Stationary Office.
10 Health and Safety Commission, *Strategic Plan for 1999/2002*, 1999, HSE Books.
11 Department of Health/Health and Safety Commission, *Healthy Workplaces – Statement of Intent*, 1998 DOH/HSC.
12 A. Giddens, *The Third Way: The Renewal of Social Democracy*, 1998, Polity Press. See also A. Giddens, *Consequences of Modernity*, 1990, Stanford.

Chapter 1

Health and safety regulation: the development of the present system

IN 1972 the Committee of Inquiry on Safety and Health at Work –
the Robens Committee – produced a report which heralded a significant change of approach in British health and safety regulation[1].
It recommended the introduction of measures which would:
- provide a more self-regulating system for health and safety;
- ensure wider coverage of those affected by the risks associated
  with work;
- clarify duties for health and safety in a single comprehensive
  framework;
- enable a greater degree of involvement of employers, workers and
  their organisations in health and safety;
- create a national authority for health and safety; and
- provide new enforcement powers to health and safety inspectors.

Prior to these recommendations the system for health and safety
regulation which had been in force in Britain was essentially one of
piecemeal prescriptive measures which were complex and sometimes incomprehensible to the people affected by them, often
marked by incomplete and overlapping coverage, produced with little involvement from either those they were intended to protect or
those whose activities they were meant to regulate, and with limited
procedures for their enforcement. It was for these reasons that the
Robens recommendations were much vaunted as a radical departure
from traditional approaches to health and safety regulation.

Such a view was not shared by all. A significant minority of critical opinion argued that the Robens approach really did very little to challenge the established pattern of regulating the creation of hazards and risks. In particular, doubt was expressed about its central argument that apathy, rather than the nature and context of work, was the primary cause of work-related injury and ill-health. Indeed, by setting so much store on the concept of self-regulation, some critics argued that its recommendations effectively eschewed the opportunity to advocate a more rigorous approach to enforcement[2]. Despite this criticism, the Robens recommendations were generally accepted by policy makers as providing a basis for the creation of a more effective system of regulation which would result in improved levels of worker protection. They were largely enacted in the Health and Safety at Work (HSW) Act 1974, which was supported by all political parties and widely held to represent a radical departure from the previous legislative strategy on health and safety when it came into force in April 1975.

Despite the considerable changes that have subsequently occurred in the nature of work and the wider society, the Act has remained the main primary legislation on health and safety in the UK to this day. Indeed, although there have been a number of changes to the framework for health and safety regulation since 1975 – occasioned by a variety of influences, such as the impact of the European Union (EU), the consequences of neo-liberalism, and changes in the structure and organisation of work and the labour market – the basic system of law has remained recognisably that introduced by the HSW Act.

The fundamental concern of this review is to consider the appropriateness is of thus system of health and safety regulation for the protection and promotion of the health and safety of people engaged in or affected by work activity. Before this question can be considered it is necessary to have some understanding of the origins and structure of the present system, and the factors which have influenced its evolution and operation over the past two decades. In addition, attention must be paid to other elements of the overall system for ensuring, in the words of the HSC, that workers are "happy, healthy and here"[3]. In particular, the means for the compensation, treatment, and rehabilitation of workers who have been harmed by their work must be considered.

The chapter begins with an outline of the framework for the regulation of health and safety that was provided by the HSW Act. It then pursues several themes which describe the impact of change on the system for health and safety regulation in this country through the 1980s and into the 1990s. Thus, it considers some of the operational and organisational influences of government strategies to reduce public expenditure and bring about the deregulation of health and safety and related areas. It also examines the influence of public opinion and the changing nature of societal perceptions of risk and its regulation, as well as the role that the compensation system plays in encouraging employers to protect their workers from harm. Finally, the chapter considers the development of the EU's role in the area of health and safety and its impact on the British system.

The HSW Act 1974 – a brief outline

THE HSW Act was intended to provide a framework through which the Robens Committee's idea of preventing injuries and ill-health through"self-regulation" could flourish. Its aim was to facilitate a shift of emphasis in British legislative provisions away from prescriptive standards towards a goal-setting approach and to create greater participation of representatives of employers and employees in the making and maintaining of preventive health and safety standards.

Under the Act a tripartite national authority was created – the Health and Safety Commission (HSC). Subsequently, a large number of industry and subject-based Joint Advisory Committees were established and a philosophy of policy making was advanced – most succinctly described in a paper by a former Director General of HSE[4] – under which, to paraphrase the Robens Report, the people who created risks and those who worked with them would be involved in decision-making about what level of risk was acceptable.

The Act also established the Health and Safety Executive (HSE) as the executive arm of the HSC with the responsibility for achieving compliance with its provisions. The HSE included a number of previously separate Inspectorates. The powers accorded to inspectors also represented a development of the previous system and allowed them greater flexibility and efficiency of enforcement action through the introduction of the right to issue enforcement notices – as well as the retention of the ability to prosecute. Penalties for offences under the Act and its Regulations were also increased from previous levels for summary offences; unlimited fines and the possibility of imprisonment were introduced for more serious offences.

The Act enables the Secretary of State to approve Regulations in which the details of the specific legislative standards can be spelt out. At the time of its introduction it did not replace the existing provisions made under previous statutes or indeed the statues themselves. Rather, it was envisaged that these earlier provisions would be replaced gradually by Regulations made under the Act. By 1999 over 80 sets of such Regulations had been introduced.

An innovation of the HSW Act was its provision for the use of Approved Codes of Practice (ACOPs), which are instruments that do not impose legal duties, but which set out the means by which a legal duty may be accomplished. ACOPs generally accompany major new sets of Regulations and their provisions relate to those in the Regulations. In the event of a breach of one of the Regulations made under the Act that is accompanied by an ACOP, the normal direction of the burden of proof is in effect reversed and the defendant required by the court to show that the means used to discharge the relevant duty were equivalent to those laid down in the ACOP.

The base requirements of the HSW Act are a set of general duties found in Sections 2 to 9. These duties cover a number of classes of persons, including employers, employees, the self employed, controllers of premises, and manufacturers and suppliers of articles and substances used at the workplace. They were intended to give everyone concerned with health and safety at work clear, concise and accessible notions of their basic legal obligations in order to remedy the criticism of the previous legislative system – that it was too complex, unwieldly and alienating to those people whose activities it was intended to regulate. They were also intended to facillitate greater attention to the management of health and safety.

The obligations on employers are detailed in Section 2. They require them to ensure the health safety and welfare of their employees. They also make clear that this duty of care extends to encompass a number of specified matters, including the provision of plant, systems of work, information, training, and supervision, means of access and egress, the working environment and the use of articles and substances. These general duties of employers, which draw on previously established common law principles, are qualified by the concept of reasonable practicability. This phrase, which appears in relation to most of the duties in the Act, draws its legal definition from case law in which it is established that the duty holder must take into account the danger or hazard or injury which may occur and balance it against the cost, inconvenience, time and trouble needed to counter it. In a much quoted case in which this legal definition was developed the judge said:

"it seems to me to imply that a computation must be made by the owner in which the quantum of risk is placed in one scale and the sacrifice involved in the measures necessary for averting the risk (whether in money, time or trouble) is placed in the other. If it be shown that there is a gross disproportion between them – the risk being insignificant in relation to the sacrifice – the defendants discharge the onus on them"

(L J Asquith in *Edwards v National Coal Board*, 1949)

That there are many problems with this qualification on the duties under the Act has become abundantly plain. It contradicts the intention of the Act to make everyone's duties clear in relation to the prevention of occupational injury and ill health, since ultimately the extent of their duty can only determined after the event, when it has been tested in court. It is also subject to differences of perception – differences which are affected by the passage of time, the extent and development of knowledge and experience and changes in societal expectation in relation to risk. Furthermore, the HSW Act's reliance on the qualification is out of step with the requirements of EU Directives and in particular with those of the EU Framework Directive 89/391 which states that

"improvements to health and safety must not be subordinated to purely economic considerations."

Employers are required further under Section 2 (3) to have a written policy in which the organisation and arrangements with which they intend to carry out their duties are identified. However, the Employers' Health and Safety Policy Statements (Exceptions) Regulations 1975 exempt employers with less than five employees from this requirement.

As well as providing the framework for a national structure of consultation over health and safety, the Act contains a statutory framework for worker representation and consultation at the level of the workplace. Thus, under Sections 2(4) and 2(7) the Secretary of State is given powers to make regulations which allow recognised trade unions to appoint safety representatives and provide such representatives with the right to require employers to set up joint health and safety committees – powers that were subsequently used to introduce the Safety Representatives and Safety Committees Regulations 1977. These measures were the only ones that precipitated any real political division during the passage of the Health and Safety at Work Bill through Parliament. It is also important to note that they were not part of the recommendations of the Robens Committee, but rather the result of a trade union campaign which had resulted in an undertaking on the part of the Labour government to introduce them.

Section 3 of the Act extended the health and safety duties of employers and the self-employed in the conduct of their undertaking to persons not in their employment. In doing so the Act provided

protection to the general public and to workers, such as sub-contractors, who are not in the direct employment of the employer in question but might be affected by the employer's activities. Further protection was afforded to these groups by Sections 4 and 5 of the Act.
Thus, the first of these sections imposes obligations on persons who
have control of non-domestic premises used as a place of work,
while the second lays down obligations on those in control of prescribed premises in respect of the emission into the atmosphere of
noxious or offensive substances[5].

The duties on the designers, manufacturers importers and suppliers of articles and substances for use at work contained in Section 6
of the Act were intended to introduce protective measures at source.
Since the Act came into force this principle has been strengthen by
amendments introduced by the Consumer Protection Act 1987. The
requirements of Section 6 are now also supplemented by European
"new approach" Directives made under Article 100A of the Treaty of
Rome.

Employees too have duties under the HSW Act. They are essentially twofold:
- a duty to take reasonable care for the health and safety of themselves and of others; and
- a duty to co-operate with employers to enable them to carry out
their statutory duties on health and safety

In addition, section 8 of the Act states that nobody should intention-
ally or recklessly interfere with or misuse anything provided in the
interests of health, safety and welfare in pursuance of relevant statutory requirements. Finally, section 9 of the Act precludes employers
from charging employees in respect of anything done or provided in
order to comply with these requirements.

The development of the statutory framework

THE development of the regulatory system following the introduction of the HSW Act occurred rather slowly for the remainder of
the 1970s, with little sign of the major revision of previous legislation
advocated by the Robens Committee. In fairness to the regulators,
the task at hand was a considerable one and the reorganisation that
had already taken place with the creation of the HSC and HSE was
itself a major development that would take time to settle in.
However, in 1979 there was a change in government. For the next 18
years a succession of Conservative governments with fundamentally
different policies to those prevalent at the time of Robens and the

passing of the HSW Act (indeed, different to those prevalent since the end of the Second World War) governed the United Kingdom. As well as pursuing a political agenda in which corporatism was rejected, trade unions attacked, institutions of the welfare state dismantled, and public expenditure massively reduced, these governments were committed to deregulatory economic strategies under which monetarism, market forces and privatisation dominated the political economy of the country.

This was indeed an extraordinary situation. Here, on the one hand, was an Act of Parliament whose development was rooted in the final stages of the tradition of British corporatism and on the other, a government with overall responsibility for its implementation and operation whose basic political and economic strategy could not have been more opposed to corporatism and its manifestations. Yet governmental edicts dismantling most of the established structures of corporatist Britain did not extend, at least directly, to the regulation of health and safety. The HSC and its IACs continued to function and there were new Regulations and ACOPs. Even the legislative rights for trade union health and safety representatives remained unscathed and their numbers, as well as government funding for their training, continued to grow well into the early 1980s. Why this was so is not clear. It is, however, probable that the 1979 Conservative government did not yet have the confidence of the support for its free market approaches to risk political damage through deregulating health and safety. It is also likely that, as far as trade union health and safety representatives were concerned, the government's anti-trade union strategies, coupled with an associated decline in trade union membership, was seen as a way of limiting the expansion of trade union safety representatives just as effectively as any overt assault on their legislative rights.

At the same time the pace with which the HSC went about introducing a new legislative framework under the HSW Act was not impressive. While it might have been anticipated that in the years immediately following the introduction of the Act progress would be slow, it is not unreasonable to expect to find evidence of significant progress by the early 1980s. This was not the case. Thus all of the major statutes that the HSW Act was designated to replace were still in force, as were the vast majority of the delegated legislation made under them. In addition, new Regulations were very few and ACOPs were hardly used. In fact activity in this area did not get underway seriously until the late 1980s and it was not until the mid-1990s that much of the old legislation was finally repealed.

The developments that occurred from the late 1980s reflected in large part the impact of three sets of influences. First, the pressures for deregulation, expenditure cuts and efficiency gains exerted by successive Conservative governments. Secondly, the advent of a large number of European directives which needed to be transposed into UK law. Thirdly, concerns arising out of a series of major disasters, such as those at Clapham Junction and Piper Alpha, and a more general change in public attitudes towards risk.

Deregulation

In 1985 and in 1986 two government White papers called for reductions in regulatory "burdens on business". Despite their targeting of health and safety regulation amongst their proposals, the legislation and the regulatory system survived subsequent scrutiny more or less intact. One reason for this was the lack of evidence that the presumed beneficiaries of deregulation, such as small firms, actually found health and safety law a burden. According to Dalton,

> "...When the government researchers went on to ask 200 small firms whether they felt health and safety law was a burden they found the requirement was not mentioned by 178 firms even when prompted"[6].

Despite the absence of widespread support for the deregulation of health and safety, later Conservative governments continued to pursue the policy. In 1993 eight high profile Deregulation Task Forces were set up under the auspices of the Department of Trade and Industry and once again health and safety regulation was a target. In addition, the Minister for Employment instructed the HSC to conduct its own review of health and safety legislation. Its brief was similar to that of the DTI Task Forces in so far as it was to review workplace health and safety legislation and advise the government on whether it was still relevant, whether it all remained necessary and whether it was possible to reduce the administrative burdens that it created for business, especially small businesses[7]. The subsequent report produced by the HSE recommended the removal of 40 per cent of the volume of health and safety legislation to reduce the "voluminous, complicated and fragmented" body of law. In particular, seven pieces of primary legislation were repealed and almost 100 sets of Regulations revoked, including most of the remaining parts of the two main Acts that regulated health and safety at work before the introduction of the 1974 Act: the Factories Act 1961 and the Offices, Shops and Railway Premises Act 1963. However, its recommendations were little more than a final acceleration of the process begun as a result of the recommendations of the Robens Committee more than 20 years before, and did not represent a challenge to the framework of law established by the HSW Act. Indeed, the HSC Review concluded that there was widespread support for maintaining the "overall architecture" of regulation. It also refrained from recommending the repeal or revocation of legislation introduced to implement EC Directives, despite the criticisms and recommendations to this effect contained in the DTI Task Force proposals. Nor did it recommend any revocation of any of the significant Regulations introduced since the 1974 Act which had been targeted by the DTI Task Forces. Furthermore, the Review found almost no support for exempting small employers or the self-employed from health and safety law. The Review, did however, recommend improving the accessibility of advice and the facilitation of public debate about the ways in which changes in the structure of employment were affecting health and safety.

The government's support for the findings of the Review indicated a move away from its previous more bullish position on the scope for reform, and suggests that by demonstrating that there was little public support for the more extreme deregulatory measures advocated elsewhere, such as the exemption of small businesses from health and safety measures, the HSC had successfully staved off major legislative reform and potential conflict with EC provisions. Particularly significant in this respect was the recommendation to leave Section 1(2) of the 1974 Act unchanged – a section which requires that new legislative provisions should provide a level of protection that is at least as rigorous as that applied previously or that which still applied to other sectors of employment[8].

However, the case against deregulation of health and safety was not won entirely. In 1994 the Deregulation and Contracting Out Act became law. This Act contains delegated powers to allow the repeal of legislation. Thus, section 37 gives the Secretary of State the "appropriate authority to repeal or revoke" any:

- provision which is an existing statutory provision for the purposes of Part 1 of the HSW Act (ie. pre-HSW Act legislation); and
- any regulatory provision made under section 15 of the HSW Act "which has effect in place of a provision which was an existing statutory provision for the purposes of that Part" (ie. Regulations made after the HSW Act which replaced pre-HSW Act legislation).

Meanwhile, in November 1995 a Deregulation Task Force, established by Michael Heseltine in the previous year to follow through the implementation of the recommendations of the eight deregulatory task forces appointed in 1993, identified health and safety legislation as "one of the single largest regulatory burdens on business".

The Task Force Report, while welcoming the HSC Review of Regulation, expressed disappointment "that some of the key Sainsbury recommendations [ie. those of the deregulatory task forces] – an urgent review of the 'six pack' of EC Directives, consolidation of legislation on flammable substances and the implementation of telephone reporting of injuries – had not yet been implemented". It also made a number of other recommendations with implications for the regulation of health and safety. For example, it recommended that a risk assessment should be required for all regulatory proposals affecting business and that the Cabinet Office be charged with providing guidance on a methodology that could be used for this purpose. It also recommended that no regulatory proposal affecting business should be entertained without a proper compliance cost assessment. For its part, the government accepted that it "should continue to discourage new EC health and safety legislation", and indicated that it was not yet finished with deregulation and that it was simply varying its approaches to the subject[9].

Pressures for efficiency and expenditure cuts

In combination these changes had significant implications for the resources, activities and policies of the HSC and HSE. Financial cut backs resulted in a decline in inspector numbers and an associated reduction in the numbers of enforcement actions and inspections undertaken[10]. Requirements on market testing within the civil service were applied to a number of peripheral areas of HSE activity – requirements which prompted fears on the part of the health and safety inspectors' trade union that they would act to both fragment the organisation and damage staff morale[11] – and major structural reorganisations resulting from wider civil service reforms led to the loss of a considerable number of senior positions and experienced staff. In addition, from 1979 onwards the HSC had to account for the economic implications of its regulatory proposals and HSE inspectors were similarly required to consider the cost-benefit implications of their enforcement actions. Indeed, new obligations were imposed on inspectors which required them to inform employers at least two weeks in advance of their intention to serve improvement notices in order to allow them time to complain to an inspector's line manager if they felt the impending notice was unjustified.

This environment of financial constrain and political hostility was, in turn, compounded by the HSE gradually acquiring new and onerous areas of enforcement responsibility (see the table below).

Major new areas of responsibility for HSE since 1974

Year	New area of responsibility	Cause
1983	Asbestos licensing	New legislation
1983	Genetic modification	New legislation
1985	Gas safety	Transfer from Dept of Energy
1985	Transport of dangerous goods by road	Transfer from police
1986	Pesticides	New legislation. Food and Environmental Protection Act
1990	Railway safety	Transfer from Department of Transport
1990	Nuclear safety research	Transfer from the Dept Energy
1991	Offshore safety	Transfer from the Dept Energy
1995	Outdoor activity centres	New licensing system

Source: 20 Years into the New Era: Some Reflections, *J. McQuaid and D. Snowball, HSE, 1995, p10*

Since the election of the present Labour government developments have been more positive. HSE funding has been increased to some extent (see chapter 3), the need for inspectors to give employers advance warning of their intention to serve an improvement notice has been removed, a consultative document entitled *Revitalising Health and Safety* has been published[12] and the establishment of a new Better Regulation Unit indicates that deregulation no longer forms a fundamental philosophical touchstone of government policy. In addition, and more generally, ministers have publicly indicated that the achievement of improved standards of workplace health and safety constitutes an important policy objective. At the same time, however, it is clear that the HSE remains seriously under-resourced[13] and that the current review of the system for health and safety at work does not extend to the carrying out of a comprehensive examination of the adequacy of the existing legal framework and the way in which it operates.

The influence of public opinion

In the period since the introduction of the HSW Act there has been a massive shift in attitudes and awareness towards the risks associated with living in contemporary Western society. In particular, environmental risks and the role of societal expectations in shaping the direction of regulatory policy in the broadest sense have become increasingly high profile issues. While this is not to say that it has necessarily resulted in any fundamental change in the nature of the governance of risk or in the relatively limited power of those affected by risks to influence their objective outcomes, it does represent a change in public consciousness and tolerance of environmental risk. This is seen, for example, in the increasing amount of both scientific and popular literature dealing with risk and risk communication[14].

Such attention has been fuelled by both subjects and the number of disasters that have occurred during the period, such as the British examples in the table below and those in other countries, notably Chernobyl, Bhopal, and Three Mile Island. However, current sociological analysis suggests that societal concern with risk runs much deeper than mere sensationalism occasioned by the reporting of a catastrophic environmental or industrial accident and is a reflection of more general trends in risk consciousness in post-industrial western societies[15].

Major incidents 1974-1992

Year	Location	Incident	Dead
1974	Flixborough	Explosion	28
1975	Appleby Frodingham	Explosion	11
1976	HMS Glasgow	Fire	8
1978	Bentley Colliery	Locomotive accident	7
1979	Golborne Colliery	Explosion	10
1984	Abbeystead	Explosion	16
1985	Putney	Domestic gas explosion	8
1985	Rutherglen	Domestic gas explosion	5
1987	Kings Cross	Fire	31
1988	Piper Alpha	Fire and exposion	167
1988	Clapham	Train crash	35
1992	Castleford	Fire	5

Source: 20 Years into the New Era: Some Reflections, *J. McQuaid and D. Snowball, HSE, 1995, p9*

Certainly, it is clear that during the 1980s and 1990s there has been:
- a growing intolerance of risk on the part of the public;
- a shift from concern about worker health and safety per se to a wider concern about the impact of business activity on the public;
- an increased readiness to press for retribution and compensation;
- increased public expectation of access to information, and demands for transparency and accountability; and
- greater demand for public involvement in decision-making processes affecting public safety.

This growth of concern with public safety led the former Director General of the HSE to estimate that by 1995 it was spending nearly half of its annual resources on this area as opposed to worker protection[16].

The development of the EU role in regulating health and safety

It is possible to discern three phases in the development of European legislation and policy on health and safety. All have influenced the British scene to some extent.

The first phase was already underway by the time the United Kingdom acceded to membership of the Community in 1972. Occupational health and safety formed part of the original objectives of European economic co-operation was established by virtue of the Treaty of Rome in 1957. Both Articles 100 and 118 of this Treaty were taken to allow for the introduction of provisions on health and safety, if they were agreed unanimously by the Council of Ministers. In fact, several directives, such as the Directive on the classification, labelling and packaging of dangerous substances, had been adopted through this process prior to the HSW Act.

In 1974 the Council initiated a social action programme that included specific reference to health and safety and which stimulated new Directives on safety signs, and vinyl chloride monomer. It also led to the establishment of the Advisory Committee on Safety Hygiene and Health Protection at Work, which became the main forum in which employers, trade unions and representatives of national authorities debated the development of detailed policy on health and safety in Europe. In 1978 the first Action Programme on health and safety was announced. The most significant legislation made under this programme was a framework Directive on the control of chemical physical and biological agents at work, known as the "harmful agents directive" (80/610/EEC, later amended by 88/642/EEC), which led to the introduction of the Control of Substances Hazardous to Health Regulations 1998. It also led to further directives on asbestos, lead and noise, all of which were implemented in British regulations in the late 1980s. A second Action Programme followed in 1984 extending the areas covered by the first.

Despite the significance of the "harmful agents directive", legislative progress within the Council of Ministers was slow, the requirement for unanimity effectively giving individual member states the opportunity to veto new requirements – an activity in which the representatives of the United Kingdom government played no small part. This changed in 1986 as a result of the Single European Act, which heralded a new phase of European level action. This Act inserted a new Article 118A into the Treaty of Rome which stated that:

"1 The Member states shall pay particular attention to encouraging improvements, especially in the working environment, as regards the health and safety of workers, and shall set as their objective the harmonisation of conditions in this area while maintaining the improvements.

2 In order to help achieve the objective laid down in the first paragraph, the Council acting by a qualified majority on a proposal from the Commission and after consulting with the European Parliament and the Economic and Social Committee, shall adopt, by means of Directives, minimum requirements for gradual implementation, having regard to the conditions and technical rules obtaining in each of the Member States..."

The provision for qualified majority voting on health and safety meant that under the third Action Programme adopted in 1987 it was possible to introduce an ambitious legislative agenda at the European level in time for the completion of the single market by the end of 1992. Spearheading the resulting Directives was the EU Framework Directive (89/391/EEC) on the introduction of measures to encourage improvements in the safety and health of workers at work. It was followed by a series of daughter directives including those on workplaces (89/655/EEC), the use of work equipment (89/655/EEC), the use of personal protective equipment (898/656/EEC), manual handling of loads (90/269/EEC), and display screen equipment (90/270/EEC) – which, along with the Framework Directive, were implemented in the UK as the "six pack regulations". Amongst further Directives adopted under the same programme were ones on temporary or mobile construction sites (92/57 EEC), implemented by the Construction (Design and Management) Regulations 1994; on pregnant workers (92/85/EEC), which led to amendments to the Management of Health and Safety at Work Regulations; on the packaging and labelling of dangerous substances, (for example, 92/32/EEC, 93/69/EEC and 93/90/EEC), which required new Chemical (Hazard Information and Packaging) Regulations (CHIP 1 and CHIP 2); on carcinogens (90/394/EEC), which required amendments to COSHH and on genetically modified organisms (90/219/EEC), implemented by the GMO (Contained Use) Regulations 1992 and 1993.

Another change to the Treaty of Rome introduced by the Single European Act was Article 100A . This allowed the Council to adopt measures for the approximation of member states' provisions and laws concerning the establishment and functioning of the internal market. It resulted in the so called "new approach" product Directives which deal with essential safety requirements and which are supported by detailed standards issued by the European standards organisations CEN and CENELEC. Such Directives have included the machinery Directive (89/392/EEC) and the personal protective equipment Directive (89/686 EEC).

At the same time as these developments were taking place discourse at European level on social policy led to the adoption of the Community Charter of Fundamental Social Rights of Workers, (the Social Charter), which contained principles on workplace health protection, safety and improved working conditions. These princniples were subsequently incorporated into a further Social Action Programme, which contained the original proposals for Directives on working time, pregnant workers and young workers. The powers of the EU to take action in the area of social policy were subsequently further increased via the Protocol on Social Policy annexed to the 1991 Maastricht Treaty. This protocol provided an alternative route for the making of European legislation on social and employment issues, including health and safety, for the member states who were signatories. That is all the then member states other than the UK. However, following the present government's decision to reverse the UK's 'opt out' from the protocol, it, as well as an amended Article 118A, has been incorporated, in a modified form, into the consolidated European Communities Treaty by mean of the Amsterdam Treaty. To what extent it will in practice be used as a channel for the development of health and safety related directives remains to be seen. It does, however, provide a means through which health and safety issues can be addressed in broader-based directives concerned with laying down requirements on working conditions and work organisation.

The period of intense legislative activity and proactive policy on the part of the EU and its institutions came to an end before the middle of the 1990s. Later years have witnessed the growth of deregulatory pressures within the EU. The result has been the adoption of far fewer directives, and those that have been adopted are unlikely to do much to improve health and safety standards. For example, the working time Directive, the protection of young people at work Directive and the pregnant workers Directive are all relatively weak and heavily qualified measures that fall far short of the systematic standards characterised by the earlier provisions. In addition, several proposals for directives have remained deadlocked at various stages within the EU bureaucracy, while others remain mere suggestions. This retreat from action is also reflected in a number of other developments. For example, the current Action Programme from the Commission was adopted three years late and centres around non-legislative measures that fall short of the joint proposals put forward by employers and trade unions. The recent establishment of the European Health and Safety Agency was also delayed for five years. Originally planned for 1992 it did not become operational until 1997. Resources for health and safety have also suffered considerable restriction, with, for example, the SAFE Programme remaining blocked by the Council following the release of limited funds in 1997[17].

Furthermore, during this third phase of EU activity various initiatives have considered the deregulation of health and safety provisions. For example, in 1995 an Anglo-German Deregulation Group, in line with the policies pursued by the then British government, called for the deregulation of a number of health and safety Directives[18]. A short while later the Commission's own Molitor Group criticised the role of EU Directives for adding obstacles to employment creation and proposed the deregulation of some measures, such as the display screen equipment Directive[19]. Although the Molitor Group's proposals did not lead to such action, it was symptomatic of the growing reaction to EU legislation on health and safety. Recent proposals in relation to employment further characterise the deregulatory flavour of EU policy in this third phase by stressing the need for increased labour market flexibility and the promotion of private enterprise and recommending the review of existing health and safety directives and the carrying out of impact assessments on future proposals[20].

The influence of the EU on the development of British health and safety legislation

The phase of action at the European level that culminated in the spate of Directives that followed the 1989 Framework Directive was an enormous influence on both the content and quantity of British health and safety legislation during the first half of the 1990s. Indeed, while British interpretation and implementation of European Directives may sometimes have been idiosyncratic and arguably often incomplete, they have become undoubtedly the single most significant source of new health and safety legislation in the country.

Analysing the influence of the thinking behind EU legislation on the national position and vice versa is a complicated affair. In the case of health and safety it is clear that British regulatory policymakers already had a view on goal-setting and self-regulation informed by their administration of the HSW Act. It is also clear that risk assessment was evolving a particularly British definition, influenced partly by the discourse behind the earlier Directives and

Regulations on biological, chemical and physical hazards, but also by debates on technical risk analysis in major hazardous industries and the development of the HSE's philosophy on the tolerability of risk. At the same time the political climate was one in which government was determined to limit as far as possible the extent of legislative change undertaken to implement EU Directives. Indeed the HSC stated, in relation to the Framework Directive that its strategy was:

"to propose regulations which meet the directive but which generally do not go beyond it, so as to minimise the impact of alterations in the law..."[21]

A leaked document from the management executive of HSE was somewhat more forthright:

"We agree that we should not seek 100% cast iron conformity with the Directive and would indeed be unable to claim that the proposals to be put to the HSC would achieve this. In fact they represent very much a minimalist approach... There is also scope in preparing the implementing regulations to do less rather than more... Thus we are proposing regulations only where they appear to be unavoidable. We are prepared to take a risk over several parts of the Directive."[22]

The Framework Directive was implemented in the UK through the provisions of the Management of Health and Safety at Work Regulations 1992, which reflect the minimalist approach to which the HSE referred, and hence provided a somewhat restrictive interpretation of its requirements. Indeed, to find evidence of the full extent to which the vision of the Framework Directive is, or is not, reflected in the British legal framework it is necessary to look beyond the implementing legislation itself and consider the provisions of the ACOP which accompanies the Regulations, and more significantly, examine the guidance on health and safety management published by the HSE.

In this guidance employers and managers are encouraged to regard health and safety management as a core business activity, managed with the same degree of commitment, expertise and to the same standards as other core business activities. The HSE suggests that the key elements of health and safety management include:

- effective health and safety policies that set a clear direction for the enterprise;
- effective management structure and arrangements in place for delivering the policy;
- a planned and systematic approach to the implementation of health and safety policy through an effective health and safety management system which includes the use of systematic risk

assessment to set priorities for eliminating hazards and reducing risks;

● measurement of performance against agreed standards to determine the functional effectiveness of the health and safety management system; and a

● systematic review of performance based on data from monitoring and the independent auditing of the whole health and safety management system with reference to key performance indicators and external comparison with the performance of business competitors and best practice[23].

Thus HSE advice embraces the EU Framework Directive, the goal-setting of the HSW Act, and the Robens approach, together with an emphasis on the economic advantages of good health and safety management. These non-legislative strategies for the management of health and safety within enterprises, which have been advocated by the HSE since the early 1990s, have risk assessment as their central focus, within a broader context of policies, structures, plans, measurement and review that bear all the hallmarks of the wider interpretation of health and safety management which is implicit in the Framework Directive. At the same time, however, the regulations that actually implement the Directive focus almost entirely on a technical interpretation of risk assessment and hence reflect a rather narrower conceptualisation of health and safety management.

A further illustration of how the British interpretation of the requirements of the Framework Directive was most powerfully influenced by the desire to "minimise the impact of alterations in the law" and "do less rather than more" is seen in the approach adopted to prevention services in the implementation of its requirements. Thus, the use of such services remains, with a few exceptions, at the discretion of employers. Similarly, their composition, as well as the qualifications of their personnel has also been left largely to employers, the market and the professional bodies to determine.

HSE spokespeople have argued that it was a desire to emphasise the importance of the management function in health and safety and to avoid encouraging the notion that management solutions can be found solely in the quality of the expert advice it employs[24] that led it to adopt a voluntary approach to the use of prevention services. Such an explanation is, however, disingenuous in the extreme when viewed in the face of the above quotations from HSC/HSE and the anti-regulatory attitude of the then Conservative government. In fact, there seems little doubt that the restricted nature of current legislative requirements is far less the product of a desire to emphasise the management function and far more the result of government determination to minimise the impact of EU Directives on the existing British system[25]. In this respect it is interesting to note that although the present government's Green Paper on a Healthier Nation is not explicit with regard to preventive services in occupational health and safety, there are some indications that it might represent a first step towards legislative change in this area.

If the early 1990s represented a watershed in terms of the regulatory influence of EU, the second half of the decade is probably best described as a period of embedding of the EU influence into the British legislative scene, which at least until the election of the present government in May 1997, was driven by a political philosophy and approach to regulation which was quite antagonistic to that which had informed the creation of the EU Directives. The position since 1997 is not radically different, although this is in part due to the influence of the grip of neo-liberalism at EU level. However, there are some differences discernable and they provide important indicators for future development. The most significant of these are found in the small but increasing number of adopted Directives which reflect wider concerns about work and its organisation than the traditional technical health and safety Directives. Thus, Directives such as the working time Directive, the protection of young persons Directive and the temporary workers Directive suggest, despite their many flaws and weaknesses, that the health and safety consequences of the organisation of work may be increasingly addressed by controls which are derived from EU social legislation. The present government seems to be adopting a relatively positive attitude towards such measures (witness its positive espousal of "family friendly" measures in employment legislation[26]). Whether this positive attitude will, however, extend to ensuring that the merging of health and safety and broader social legislation is achieved through measures that are really effective remains to be seen.

Compensation and the prevention of harm

In its report the Robens Committee did provide some discussion of the extent to which the Industrial Injuries Scheme (IIS) and common law actions for damages provided employers with an incentive to prevent work-related harm. However, it did not feel that its terms of reference allowed it to examine the operation of the compensation system in detail or to put forward recommendations for change. Nevertheless, it did make two recommendations. First, that a detailed study should be undertaken as to the possibility of amending the IIS to introduce differential rates of employers' contributions based on claims experience. Secondly, that a review should be conducted of the system of actions for damages at common law, with particular reference to the effects of the system upon accident-prevention provisions and arrangements.

Subsequently, a review of civil law compensation was commenced in the late 1970s by the Pearson Commission. In its report this Commission did recommend changes to both the IIS and the operation of the tort system[27]. It did not, however, support the reform of the IIS along the lines raised by the Robens Committee. Nor did it favour utilising the system of employers' liability insurance to provide employers with an incentive to encourage them to do more to stop worker injuries and ill health. Recent changes to the operation of the tort system stemming from the Woolf report have also not done anything to encourage it to influence employers to do more to prevent work-related harm[28], while the withdrawal of legal aid from personal injury actions may result in such actions being utilised by an even smaller proportion of those harmed through their work activities[29].

As a result, since its inception, the HSW Act has not been effectively supported by a compensation system which supports effectively its preventive objectives. As shall be seen in chapter 5, this situation contrasts sharply with the position in a number of other countries. Indeed, in some national systems preventive activity on the part of employers is further encouraged by the imposition of obligations on them regarding the organisation and funding of worker rehabilitation.

Recently, however, there have been signs that the present government is concerned to adopt a more holistic approach to reform. Thus, the Department of Social Security has examined the scope for reforming the industrial injuries scheme to support a closer integration between compensation, prevention and rehabilitation. There has also been recognition of the need for further "joined up" thinking between government departments, the insurance industry, the social partners and the legal profession to ensure that workers do not leave the workforce prematurely[30].

Conclusion

IN this chapter we have tried to do two things. First, we have described the broad infrastructure of the system for health and safety regulation in Britain, its policy underpinnings and its development during the past twenty-five years. Secondly, we have considered some of the influences on both its operation and development during this period.

The discussion has highlighted how the HSW Act, the core of the

current regulatory system, was in large part based on the recommendations put forward in the 1972 report of the Robens Committee. It
has also drawn attention to the fact that the Act esesentially sought,
notably by the laying down of broad, goal-orientated, general duties
on employers and others, and the establishment of a framework for
worker representation, to create a legal system which encouraged
greater self-regulation on the part of employers and workers: albeit
one that also provided more extensive enforcement powers to
inspectors.

It has also been shown that for much of its life the framework of
law established by the HSW Act has, at the domestic national level,
operated in a hostile political environment. In particular, successive
Conservative governments cut the funding of the HSE, increasingly
required regulatory proposals and enforcement action to be justified
in cost-benefit terms and exerted on-going pressures for deregulation. However, while these pressures led to the repeal and revocation
of a substantial body of existing law, they did not act to fundamentally reduce the statutory obligations of employers. Rather they can
better be seen as having stimulated the overhaul of pre-HSW Act
legislation along the lines advocated by the Robens Committee.

In fact, as a result of a growth in European level activity in respect
of health and safety, a raft of new regulations were made in order to
transpose into domestic law the requirements of new directives. This
expansion of European-inspired legislation inevitably caused concerns for Conservative governments committed to a deregulatory
agenda. These concerns were, in part, addressed by the adoption of
an often minimalist approach to the transposition of directives – an
approach most clearly seen in the inadequate way in which the HSC
sought to implement the requirements of the framework directive
relating to preventive health and safety services and the management
of health and safety more generally.

At the same time, not withstanding these domestic and European
developments, the HSW Act remained largely unaltered, as did the
self-regulatory philosophy which underlay it. That this was the case
could be seen to illustrate the stengths of the regulatory system put
in place by the Act and the soundness of the Robens analysis on
which it was largely based. On the other hand, it could also be seen
to reflect a misguided faith in the systemn's adequacy on the part of
the health and safety establishment. In the pages that follow we will
shed light on the validity of these alternative explanations.

Notes

1   Lord Robens (1972) *Safety and Health at Work: Report of the Committee 1970-72*, Cmnd. 5034, 1972.

2   For example see, T. Nichols and P. Armstrong, *Safety or Profit?* Falling Wall Press, 1973, A. Woolf, "The Robens Report – the Wrong Approach", *Industrial Law Journal*, 1973, 2, 88-95. For a more recent discussion see S. Dawson, P. Willman, M. Bamford, and A. Clinton, (1988) *Safety at work: The limits of self regulation,* Cambridge University Press, Cambridge, and in the context of the relevance of self-regulation to hazards in the chemical industry see D. Smith and S. Tombs, "Beyond Self-Regulation: Towards a Critique of Self-Regulation as a Control Strategy for Hazardous Activities", *Journal of Management Studies*, 32, 1995, 619-636.

3   DETR/HSC (1999) *Revitalising Health and Safety,* Consultation Document, DETR, London.

4   J. Locke, (1981) *The Politics of Health and Safety,* Sir Alexander Redgrave Memorial Lecture, IOSH; also summarised in Protection, July 1981.

5   No premises have so far been prescribed for the purposes of this regulation.

6   A.J.P. Dalton (1992) Lessons from the United Kingdom: Fightback on workplace hazards, *International Journal of Health Services,* vol 22, No 3 pp. 489-495,

7   HSC (1994) *Review of Health and Safety Regulations,* HSE Books, Sudbury

8   Hendy, J. (1994) *International Trade and International Trade Union and Workers' Rights,* 1st Jack Hendy Memmorial Lecture, Thames Valley University.

9   H. Fidderman, (1998) Mood music with Jenny Bacon, *Health and Safety Bulletin* No 266, pp. 10-15, IRS and H. Fidderman, 1998 More HSE mood music, *Health and Safety Bulletin*, 266, pp 7-12, IRS.

10 P. James, (1997) The enforcement record of the HSE's Field Operations Division, *Health and Safety Bulletin,* No 261, pp. 9-12, IRS.

11 IPMS (1993) *Health and Safety: Keep it Together,* Institute of Professionals, Managers and Specialists, London.

12 see note 3

13 see notes 8 and 9

14 Royal Society (1992) *Risk: analysis, perception and management: Report of a Royal Society study group,* The Royal Society, London; Adams, J. (1995) *Risk,* UCL Press, London.

15 U. Beck, (1992) *Risk Society: Towards a New Modernity,* Trans M. Ritter, Sage London

16 J. Rimington, *Valedictory summary of industrial health and safety since the 1974 Act,* paper presented at the Electricity Association 26/4/1995 (summarised in Health and Safety Bulletin, 236 August 1995, pp. 11).

17 L. Vogel, (1998) The TUTB Observatory on the application of the European Directives: preliminary assessment *TUTB Newsletter* No. 8 pp. 4-9, TUTB, Brussels.

18 Commission of the European Community (1995) *Report of the Group of Independent Experts on the Simplification of Legislation and Administration* COM (95), 288 final/2.

19 European Trade Uniion Technical Bureau for Health and Safety (1995) *TUTB Newsletter* No. 1, pp. 2-3 Molitor Group: deregulation assault on health and safety, Oct 95, Brussels.

20 M. Sapir, (1998) A fragile balance under threat? Editorial, *TUTB Newsletter*

No. 9 pp. 1-2, Also M. Sapir, The BEST report: employment law deregulation moves one step closer, *TUTB Newsletter* No. 9 pp 11-14 Brussels.

21 HSC (1991) proposals for Health and Safety (General Provisions) Regulations and Approved code of practice, Consultation Document, HMSO.

22 M. Everley, (1993) Leaked letter causes rumpus over HSE risk-taking, *The Safety and Health Practitioner,* January

23 HSE (1997) *Guide to Successful Health and Safety Management,* (2nd ed.) HSG65, HSE Books, Sudbury

24 T. Carter, (1997) An HSE perspective on occupational health, *Occupational Health Review,* No. 69, September/October, pp. 32-35. IRS.

25 In response to pressure from the European Commission, regulations introducing some changes to the MHSW Regulations to clarify the UK's implementation of the Framework Directive were proposed in 1999. If implemented they would include some tightening of the employers' obligations to use competent health and safety personnel which would help to bring the UK more in line with the Directive but would still fall considerably short of requirements in many EU countries. HSE (1999) *Proposals for the Health and Safety (Miscellaneous Modifications) Regulations 1999 and the Ammendment of the MHSW Approved Code of Practice,* Consultation Document 142, HSE, London.

26 White paper: *Fairness at Work,* Dept. Trade and Industry, HM Stationary Office 1998

27 Pearson (1978) *Report of the Royal Commission on Civil Liability and Compensation for Personal Injury* Cmnd. 7054, 1978

28 Croner (1999) Woolf reforms: new civil procedure rules, *Health and Safety Briefing* No. 167, pp. 4-5.

29 S. Pickvance, (1997) Employers' liability – a system of balance, *Occupational Health Review* Sept/Oct 1997, pp. 1-4

30 see note 3

Chapter 2

Employers and their statutory duties

OCCUPATIONAL health and safety legislation has always focused primarily on the role that employers and the occupiers of work premises play in ensuring adequate standards of worker protection. The self-regulatory philosophy advocated by the Robens Committee, and given statutory effect by the HSW Act, continued to emphasise this role and with good reason. For it is the employer who ultimately controls work activities and the organisational and physical environment within which they take place. Indeed it was precisely this feature of working life that led Robens to stress the importance of using the law to encourage greater self-regulation on the part of both employers and workers.

In this chapter attention is consequently paid to the adequacy of current employer approaches towards the management of health and safety at work and how far they appear to be embracing the central tenets of self-regulation. Initially, the meaning of self-regulation and the managerial practices considered central to its effective operation are considered. The operation of self-regulation in practice is then explored in relation to the legal duties placed on employers through a consideration of three issues: the willingness of employers to develop and implement the organisational arrangements necessary to ensure the health and safety of workers; the extent to which they have the capability to both establish and effectively operate such arrangements; and the degree to which current management systems and practices do currently act to protect workers from work-related harm.

The meaning of self-regulation

IN its report the Robens Committee did not provide a comprehensive model of what constituted effective self-regulation on the
part of employers. Rather, the committee identified and discussed
three "prerequisites" which it considered were needed if "progress
towards a more effectively self-regulating system" was to be
achieved[1]. First, awareness of the importance of the issue, particularly at the senior management level. Secondly, the clear definition of
organisational responsibilities. Thirdly, the methodical assessment of
the nature of problems and the translation of these assessments into
practical objectives and courses of action.

Subsequently the HSW Act sought to establish a legislative framework that would encourage the more widespread adoption of these
"prerequisites" through the imposition of three sets of duties on
employers. First, the duty laid down under section 2(1) to ensure, so
far as is reasonably practicable, the health, safety and welfare at work
of all employees: a duty which section 2(2) makes clear encompasses
responsibilities with regard to a number of specific matters, such as
the provision and maintenance of systems of work, arrangements
relating to the use, handling, storage and transport of articles, and
the provision of information, instruction, training and supervision.
Secondly, the requirements under section 2(3) to prepare a written
statement of health and safety policy and the organisation and
arrangements in place to implement this policy, to bring this statement to the attention of employees, and to periodically review, and
where necessary, revise it. Thirdly, the laying down of a duty under
section 3 to ensure, again so far as is reasonably practicable, the
health and safety of non-employees who might be affected by an
undertaking's activities.

Later regulations and associated ACOPs, as well as a wide-range
of official guidance material, have added further detail to what
employers need to do to protect workers, and in doing so served to
specify more clearly the types of management and preventive
arrangements that they need to put in place. In recent years many of
these regulations have been introduced to implement the requirements of EC directives – although the extent to which they have in
fact done so has been variable[2]. For example, as a result of such
directives new regulatory requirements have been introduced in
respect of the carrying out of risk assessments and the implementation of their results, the appointment of competent persons, and the
provision of both information and training, and workforce consultation. Indeed the Management of Health and Safety at Work
(MHSW) Regulations 1992, a set of regulations introduced to imple-

ment two EC directives – the safety framework directive and that on temporary workers – cover all of these matters and as a result effectively provide a far clearer statutory outline of what self-regulation is than do the duties imposed under sections 2 and 3[3].

More generally, the HSE, through a series of publications produced during the 1980s and the early part of this decade, such as *Managing Safety* in 1981, *Monitoring Safety* in 1985, *Human Factors in Industrial Safety* in 1989 and *Organising for Safety* in 1993, has spelt out in some detail the main issues that need to be considered by employers when approaching the management of health and safety. Much of this guidance was brought together by the HSE in the booklet *Successful Health and Safety Management* (HS(G)65), a publication first issued in 1991, and subsequently revised in 1997[4]. HS(G)65 therefore provides the most comprehensive official outline of what constitutes effective self-regulation on the part of employers.

Successful Health and Safety Management

The Foreword to *HS(G)65*, describes the document as setting out the "main elements of successful health and safety management" and goes on to state that it "is designed to be a source of reference and guidance to all those involved in the management system – general managers, those with special health and safety responsibilities and people at the very top of organisations". Moreover, it can "be used to develop programmes for improvement, define training needs and audit performance".

These programmes are viewed in close connection to other management initiatives. The document states that "much of the guidance involves the application of the principles of total quality management to health and safety... Good health and safety management, like good human resource management generally, is something to which many organisations aspire; it is also something which the law requires". It further argues that not only does health and safety management form a part of modern management, but that there is a clear business case for it. Hence, it is noted that the costs of failure to manage health and safety successfully can be so high that they constitute "the difference between profit and loss".

Underlying the HSE's approach is the assumption that "losses, whether counted in human or financial terms, are not inevitable and experience has shown that real and substantial improvements can be achieved by applying the guidance in this publication". Indeed, the authors of *HS(G)65* view the guidance given in their publication as a near fail-safe recipe for success. Thus they state:

"each chapter provides points of reference for the various stages in developing a successful health and safety management system - starting with effective well-considered policies of organising, planning and going right through to methods of auditing and reviewing performance. HSE inspectors will be using this publication as a guide when judging the adequacy of health and safety management and compliance with statutory requirements."

More specifically, HS(G)65 makes the following observations regarding health and safety policies, the organisation and planning of health and safety management, and the monitoring, auditing and reviewing of health and safety performance:

Policy

Organisations which are successful in achieving high standards of health and safety have health and safety policies which contribute to their business performance, while meeting their responsibilities to people and the environment in a way which fulfils both the spirit and the letter of the law. In this way, they satisfy the expectations of shareholders, employees, customers and society at large. Their policies are cost effective and aimed at achieving the preservation and development of physical and human resources and reductions in financial losses and liabilities. Their health and safety policies influence all their activities and decisions, including those to do with the selection of resources and information, the design and operation of working systems, the design and delivery of products and services, and the control and disposal of waste.

Organisation

Organisations which achieve high health and safety standards are structured and operated so as to put their health and safety policies into effective practice. This is helped by the creation of a positive culture which secures involvement and participation at all levels. It is sustained by effective communications and the promotion of competence which enables all employees to make a responsible and informed contribution to the health and safety effort. The visible and active leadership of senior managers is necessary to develop and maintain a culture supportive of health and safety management. Their aim is not simply to avoid accidents, but to motivate and empower people to work safely. The vision, values and beliefs of leaders become the shared "common knowledge" of all.

Planning

These successful organisations adopt a planned and systematic approach to policy implementation. Their aim is to minimise the risks created by work activities, products and services. They use risk assessment methods to decide priorities and set objectives for hazard elimination and risk reduction. Performance standards are established and performance is measured against them. Specific actions needed to promote a positive health and safety culture and to eliminate and control risks are identified. Wherever possible, risks are eliminated by the careful selection and design of facilities, equipment and processes or minimised by the use of physical control measures. Where this is not possible, systems of work and personal protective equipment are used to control risks.

Measuring performance

Health and safety performance in organisations which manage health and safety successfully, is measured against pre-determined standards. This reveals when and where action is needed to improve performance. The success of action taken to control risks is assessed through active self-monitoring involving a range of techniques. This includes an examination of both hardware (premises, plant and substances) and software (people, procedures and systems), including individual behaviour. Failures of control are assessed through reactive monitoring which requires the thorough investigation of any accidents, ill health or incidents with the potential to cause harm or loss. In both active and reactive monitoring the objectives are not only to determine the immediate causes of sub-standard performance but, more importantly, to identify the underlying causes and the implications for the design and operation of the health and safety management system.

Auditing and reviewing performance

Learning from all relevant experience and applying the lessons learned, are important elements in effective health and safety management. This needs to be done systematically through regular reviews of performance based on data both from monitoring activities and from independent audits of the whole health and safety management system. These form the basis for self-regulation and for securing compliance with Sections 2 to 6 of the Health and Safety at Work etc. Act 1974. Commitment to continuous improvement involves the constant development of policies, approaches to implementation and techniques of risk control. Organisations which achieve high standards of health and safety assess their health and safety performance by internal reference to key performance indicators and by external comparison with the performance of business competitors. They often also record and account for their performance in their annual reports.

Overall, then, HS(G)65 can be seen to lay down a comprehensive and proactive approach to the management of health and safety and in doing so echoes the lessons and findings of many research studies and official inquiries (see below). At the same time, it is also clear that this approach is premised on a number of key assumptions, namely:

- people are an organisation's most important asset;
- the preservation of human and physical resources is an important means of minimising costs;
- the majority of accidents and incidents are not caused by 'careless workers', but by failures in control (either within the organisation or within the particular job), which are the responsibility of management;
- health and safety is a management responsibility of equal importance to production and quality;
- effective control of health and safety is achieved through co-operative effort at all levels in the organisation. Effective health and safety management is not "common sense" but is based on a common understanding of risks and how to control them brought about through good management;
- competence in managing health and safety is an essential part of professional management;
- all accidents, ill health and incidents are preventable;
- health and safety, and quality, are two sides of the same coin.

In combination these assumptions – or as HSE, perhaps, tellingly refers to them, "beliefs" – can be seen to suggest that (a) employers have a financial incentive to adequately manage health and safety and (b) that they possess the ability to do so. Unfortunately, research evidence which sheds light on the willingness and capacity of employers to effectively manage health and safety, casts grave doubt on the validity of both these propositions[5].

Employer willingness

THE business case for health and safety advanced in HS(G)65 can be seen to fit uneasily with the qualification of the employer's duty in section 2(1) of the HSW Act in terms of reasonably practicability. For this qualification serves to require the courts to balance the scale of risk on the one hand against the time and resources required to control the risk on the other[6]. In effect therefore section 2(1) acknowledges that there is a point where it becomes "uneconomic" to remove existing risks.

How far employers do experience, or perceive, a conflict between health and safety expenditure and the achievement of other organisational goals is unclear. However, there are good grounds for believing that such conflict is the norm rather than the exception.

In its report *The Costs of Accidents* the HSE, through the medium of five case studies, sought to demonstrate the large-scale costs incurred by employers through accidents deemed "economic to prevent"[7]. In doing so it went on to again argue that there is a strong economic case for employers to do more to prevent such events. The exclusion of accidents that were considered not economic to prevent, however, demonstrates once again that there are clear limits to the business case. Moreover, even if this issue is ignored, the fact remains that the costs of accident study does not, even on its own terms, clearly demonstrate that the case study organisations had an economic incentive to invest further on health and safety[8]. Thus, no account is taken of the potential opportunity costs associated with this expenditure. In addition, no recognition is given to the fact that while organisations might recognise the long-term benefits of a given expenditure, their ability to make it might be hindered by short-term budgetary and financial constraints, and the internal politics of management decision-making processes is ignored with the result that it is questionably assumed that organisations invariably behave in an economically rationale way.

Furthermore, the findings of official inquiries conducted into the causes of major disasters, such as Piper Alpha, the sinking of the Zeebrugge and the Clapham Junction accident, add weight to the above doubts about the extent to which employers view the maintenance of high standards of health and safety as integral to their financial performance. For example, the Zeebrugge inquiry found that the immediate cause of the sinking was the failure of an Assistant Bosun to close the bow doors prior to sailing[9]. It further discovered, however, that the possibility of such an occurrence had been raised previously to senior management with a request that indicator lights be used to confirm that the doors were closed. This request was, however, rejected with one manager responding "don't we already pay someone?". In a similar vein Lord Cullen, the chair of the Piper Alpha inquiry, expressed puzzlement as to why, with so much construction and maintenance work taking place, it had been decided to allow production to continue[10], while the Clapham Junction inquiry found that an internal memo written by a senior BR manager had earlier drawn attention to how a new system for appraising investment decisions provided an "organisational disincentive for health and safety", and concluded that a contributory factor to the accident was the decision to carry out a re-signalling project to a deadline which could only be met by staff working exceptionally long hours[11].

Disasters of the scale of Zeebrugge, Piper Alpha and Clapham Junction are of course exceptional in terms of the scale of the harm involved. A host of other studies, however, also demonstrate how operational pressures stemming from production and broader financial objectives can act to endanger the health and safety of workers. For example, piecework payment systems, intended to encourage workers to produce more, have been found to be associated with higher accident levels[12]; several pieces of research have, relatedly, found evidence of an association between accident rates and work intensity[13]; the interim findings of a recent HSE-funded survey reveal strong associations between perceived levels of stress and such factors as working long hours, high exposure to noise, having to work fast and high workloads[14]; and a recent study showed how the desire to reduce energy and running costs can lead to the design of office environments with lighting, heating and ventilation arrangements that result in workers suffering adverse health effects[15]. HSE commissioned research into the links between total quality and health and safety management, two processes which, as has been seen, are considered in HS(G)65 to be mutually supporting, merely serves to further highlight the relatively low importance often accorded to worker protection. For the researchers not only found that these links were often limited but further concluded that this lack of linkage partly stemmed from a leadership vacuum at executive level in respect of health and safety and a view that investment in health and safety does not generate income or profits[16].

The view that health and safety is accorded a relatively low priority by British employers is furthermore supported by the findings of a series of other HSE funded studies which reveal that many of them remain unaware of their legal obligations and hence are unlikely to be complying with them. A case in point is a recent study conducted to evaluate the impact of the 1992 "six-pack regulations" which found that only 43% had heard of the MHSW regulations and that awareness of the other five sets of regulations, although higher, was still far from impressive – the relevant percentages ranging from 50% to 71%[17]. More graphically, a recent prosecution of J Sainsbury's plc, following the death of a warehouse worker, for various offenses, including breaches of section 2 of the HSW and various provisions of the MHSW regulations and the Provision and Use of Work Equipment Regulations 1992, demonstrates that even some of the country's largest employers adopt a cavalier approach to their legal obligations. Thus, in imposing fines on the company totalling £425,000, the judge referred to a "picture of working practices that date back to the dark ages of work safety" and also accused the supermarket chain of having priorities that meant that "making money was at the top of the list and safety was at the bottom"[18].

In short, the existing research evidence suggests that the bulk of British employers do not possess a willingness to adopt and implement the types of arrangements advocated in HS(G)65 or, more generally, to effectively self-regulate themselves. It further suggests that many of them, partly out of ignorance, do not even comply with their current legal duties.

Employer capacity

FOR effective self-regulation to occur it is clear that employers (a) need to possess the knowledge and expertise needed to identify risks and appropriate remedial strategies and (b) have in place management systems that ensure that these processes are carried out and that any necessary remedial actions are taken. Consequently, in this section attention is paid to two, related, issues. First, the extent to which the present legal framework ensures that organisations do possess the health and safety knowledge and expertise they need. Secondly, how far employers currently are able to adequately identify and control risks.

Knowledge/expertise

Under the MHSW Regulations employers are required to appoint one or more competent persons to assist them in undertaking preventive activities. A competent person for these purposes, however, is defined in very general terms as someone who has "sufficient training and experience or knowledge and other qualities to enable him to properly assist..." As a result the regulations do not require employers to have access to professionally qualified safety or occupational health specialists – a situation that contrasts sharply with that in most other member states of the European Union and almost certainly means that UK law fails to comply with the provisions of the EC framework directive on protective and preventive services[19].

Little is known about the extent to which employers have access, either internally or via outside consultancies and services, to specialist safety advisers/managers. What is known is that the current membership of the Institution of Occupational Safety and Health currently stands at around 25,000, of which only approximately 40% consists of corporate members. That is, those who have obtained the relevant professional qualifications and have three years' relevant work experience. These figures therefore suggest that only a small proportion of employers are able to draw on the knowledge and advice of individuals possessing professional qualifications in safety. A similar picture of highly partial coverage emerges if attention is paid to the use of occupational health specialists, such as occupational physicians and nurses, and hygienists by private sector employers. For example, the most recent study in this area found that only 8% of establishments either employed, or had access to, such professionals, although these establishments were estimated to employ 36% of private sector employees: a situation which contrasts sharply with the 98% coverage found in the public sector[20].

Moreover, where organisations do make use of occupational health professionals, their preventative role is often limited and, in particular, appears rarely to extend to the identification of health problems at their presymtomatic stage. Thus, the above study found that only 43% of those used by private sector establishments provided advice on health and safety measures, just 40% played a role in "identifying other areas which might cause health problems" and a slightly smaller proportion (39%) conducted regular health checks on some staff.

There is little doubt, then, that at present, health and safety in most British enterprises is carried out in the absence of specialist expertise. However, this general picture masks significant differences between sectors and sizes of undertaking. In particular, whereas 68% of establishments with 200 or more employees had some type of health professional, the corresponding figures for those employing between 25 and 199 and below 25 were 32% and 5% respectively. It is perhaps no coincidence therefore that the survey referred to above found that only 41% of organisations with less than 50 employees were aware of the MHSW, compared with 80% of those employing 50 or more.

The lack of health and safety knowledge and expertise within SMEs is of crucial importance for three reasons. First, there has been a substantial growth of employment within such enterprises to the point where over 40% of the working population is employed in businesses possessing fewer than 250 staff[21]. Secondly, there is clear evidence that workers employed in SMEs face greater risks. For example, a recent HSE study found the rates of fatal injury and injuries involving amputations in manufacturing workplaces with less than 50 employees to be twice as high as was the case in establishments that had 200 or more[22]. Thirdly, the HSC's 1994 Review of Regulation revealed that managers in SME's frequently experienced difficulties in interpreting and applying modern goal-setting statutory requirements and in doing so indicated that a more pre-scriptive approach to the drafting of statutory requirements would be preferred – an issue to which we return below[23].

Management systems and control

There seems little doubt that the HSE is correct to argue that health and safety can only be managed effectively if it is approached in both a systematic and integrated way. That such a situation is desirable does not, however, mean that it exists very often in prac-tice. Indeed the arguments already advanced concerning the willing-ness of employers to both prioritise and invest in health and safety suggest that the opposite is the case. In fact there is ample evidence to indicate that employers all too often do not adequately identify risks, or establish appropriate preventive measures to control the risks that have been identified, or ensure that these measures are fully implemented.

For present purposes the following sample "case study" examples, contained in an HSE publication entitled *Improving Compliance with Safety Procedures*, are sufficient to clearly demonstrate these last points, particularly as they relate to large organisations operating in highly hazardous environments – in other words organisations which would be expected to have a "more sophisticated" approach to the management of health and safety[24]:

Extract from the King's Cross Disaster Inquiry

"Many of the shortcomings in the physical and human state of affairs at King's Cross on 18 November 1987 had in fact been identified before by internal inquiries into escalator fires... The many recommendations had not been adequately considered by senior managers... London Underground's failure to carry through the proposals resulting from earlier fires... was a failure which I believe contributed to the disaster at King's Cross."

International Chemical Firm Fined £250,000

"A vessel used in the distillation of nitrotoluene had been in use for 25 years and had never been cleaned out. Despite professing to be experts in the field, no one at the company knew what the residues were or what had formed over that time.

A 'rocket-like jet of flames' devastated a control room and an office block at the plant after a chemical cleaning job went wrong. Although the operators were under verbal instructions not to heat the sediment above 90°, they did not locate the thermometer cor-rectly and monitored the vapour temperature above the liquid. Furthermore 'everything that should have been done to ensure safe practice was dealt with in what can only be described as a haphazard and knowingly wrong way'.

Because senior management failed to realise the complexity of the cleaning process and to issue instructions on technical expertise 'there existed a lacuna which needed to be filled by their own initiative and that's exactly what they did'".

Impractical Rules Encourage Violations

"A Code of Practice stated that no person should enter a bunker or silo unless all material adhering to the bunker sides had been removed above the point where the work had to be performed. This was a requirement to prevent vibration etc causing adhering material to fall on the people working below – a known cause of fatal accidents. Despite the obvious importance of this requirement men were still being killed in this way. When this was investigated it became apparent that there was no practical way of fulfilling the Code of Practice requirement. Workers chose to take the risk to get the job done."

Oil Rig Explosion Raises New North Sea Platform Questions

"Following an incident inquiry on an oil platform, a report identified the presence of over 1500 electrical system faults on the platform. The company confirmed that the report was accurate but said that the apparently high total was misleading as many were minor and related to faulty labelling or missing screws.

A specialist said that in his view such a degree of electrical faults would require a thorough investigation of the planned maintenance systems. He questioned the maintenance procedures and structure of supervisory arrangements both offshore and onshore that would have led to a build-up of so many faults"

These findings not only serve to raise questions about managerial motivations and competence, but also, and more generally, doubts about the extent to which health and safety can be adequately controlled through a "top down" approach to management. For they clearly show that health and safety cannot be managed effectively without workforce involvement in the processes of identifying risks, developing necessary preventive measures and monitoring the implementation of those measures. This point is admittedly to some extent acknowledged, although in a rather limited way and without sufficient emphasis on the importance of trade union involvement, in HS(G)65, which refers to the need for an effective health and safety policy to allow "all employees to make a responsible and informed contribution to the health and safety effort". However, its importance, which is discussed further in chapter 4, cannot be stressed enough.

In recent years considerable attention has been paid to the concept of **safety culture**. The HSE, for example, has produced a number of publications which deal with the issue[25]. Unfortunately, notwithstanding the plethora of publications on the subject, there is hardly any agreement on what the term means. Moreover, even if such agreement did exist, the research evidence discussed above raises major doubts about how far management is capable on its own of creating a clear safety culture. For much evidence exists to indicate that organisations frequently are not marked by one all pervasive set of values and beliefs, but rather a variety of sub-cultures that exist in a dynamic tension with each other[26]. As a result such studies highlight the fact that management attempts to unilaterally impose its own cultural assumptions may be resisted if they are seen to conflict with those held by other groups within the organisation. Indeed they suggest that management-driven culture change programmes may, by downplaying the importance of countervailing workforce views and values, actually generate conflict rather than consensus and hence ultimately be counter-productive. That this is a real danger is clearly illustrated by the following statement made by a BP spokesperson in 1992:

> "...any organisation that has a legitimate interest in safety is welcome to work with my organisation as long as they are working with the grain of what I have been describing and in a way which will add to it. But it should also be made clear that any organisation using safety to work to a different agenda will be a potential hindrance to the alignment inherent in what I have been describing."

These doubts about the feasibility of management establishing a distinct safety culture and, more generally, managing health and safety through a "top down" approach are reinforced when account is taken of the changes that have occurred over the last two decades in organisational structures and employment practices. For these have frequently involved the introduction of more devolved management structures that rely to a far greater extent on indirect and financially-based systems of control and also led to employment relationships that are more distant and transitory. Thus, activities that had previously been carried out in-house have often been sub-contracted, and far greater use has been made of various forms of "non-standard" employment, such as homeworking, self-employment, and part-time and temporary working[27].

Relatively little research has been conducted to discover how far these changes have had adverse consequences for health and safety standards in Britain. It is clear, however, that those engaged on non-standard forms of employment can be exposed to relatively high levels of risk. For example, over 20% of homeworkers interviewed in a government-funded study reported that they had suffered accidents, injuries or ill health caused by their work[28]; official accident statistics indicate that self-employed workers are twice as likely as employees to be killed at work[29]; Australian researchers have found self-employment to be associated with higher levels of injury among self-employed construction workers and lorry drivers[30]; and findings from the Second European survey of the working environment revealed that agency workers and those on fixed-term contracts were significantly more likely to undertake work involving repetitive tasks, repetitive movements and painful or tiring working positions – all factors associated with musculoskeletal disorders[31].

The performance of self-regulation

OFFICIAL accident statistics provide, at least in theory, a potential means of assessing trends in accidents since the coming into force of the HSW Act and hence a way of assessing its impact. In practice, however, a number of factors act to make such an exercise difficult, if not impossible. The most obvious is the fact that no fewer than four accident reporting (or collection) regimes have been used over the period with the result that (with the exception of figures relating to fatalities) no consistent set of data can be compiled. However, the longitudinal evaluation of accident trends is further made difficult by the fact that worker exposure to risk has changed for reasons which are unconnected to trends in standards of health and safety management, most notably the growth of "non-standard" forms of employment, the expansion of non-manual relative to manual employment, the use of more technologically advanced and safer equipment, and the shift of employment away from manufacturing and the extractive industries to the service sector. The official statistics on work-related fatalities can be used to illustrate this point.

Over the period since 1975 the number and rate of fatal accidents to employees have fallen significantly to the point where the fatal injury rate for employees in 1997/98 was a quarter of what it was in 1971[32]. This fall, which it should be noted has not been continuous, would at first glance seem to support a suggestion that safety has improved since the coming into force of the 1974 Act. When account is taken, however, of sectoral shifts in employment away from "high risk" sectors and occupations to "lower risk" ones the picture becomes less clear. Thus, in its 1994/95 annual report the HSC estimated that about half of the fall in the fatal injury rate could be attributed to shifting patterns of employment and more recently has suggested that around a third of the improvement that has occurred in the 1990s is likely to have stemmed from "changes in the structure of the economy"[33]. Yet these estimates may well still underestimate the extent to which the decline in fatal accident statistics has occurred for reasons unconnected with improved levels of safety performance on the part of employers. For they take no account of the way in which employee exposure to risk may have fallen due to changes in working hours flowing from the growth of part-time work, the "exportation of risk" to self-employed contractors, and shifts in the occupational composition of workers within, as opposed to between, sectors.

Research undertaken by Nichols indicates clearly that such factors can exert an important influence over official accident rates. Thus, in an analysis of trends in the combined fatal and major injury rate for manufacturing industry over the period 1986/87 to 1994/95 he found that the decline in this rate reported in the official statistics disappeared when the denominator on which it was based was changed from "all employees" to the total number of weekly hours worked by operatives[34]. On the basis of his findings, Nichols therefore concludes that the decline in the official rate over the period in question largely stemmed from a decrease in the number of operatives employed and an increase in the number of administrative, technical and clerical staff utilised.

As a result of these statistical difficulties it is possible for widely differing conclusions to be reached of the effectiveness of the HSW Act and the self-regulatory philosophy which underlies it. At the same time the available evidence, in our view, raises major doubts regarding the widely espoused view that the current legislative framework has led to significantly higher standards of safety and hence "stood the test of time"[35].

These doubts are moreover given added weight when attention is paid to the current extent of work-related harm suffered by workers. Official accident statistics, for example, show that 212 employees, 62 self-employed workers and 127 members of the public died as a result of work-related accidents during 1997/98 – a grand total of 401 deaths. They further show that between them these groups suffered 194,388 non-fatal accidents[36].

These figures are obviously large. However, they provide a far from full picture of the present situation. The fatal accident statistics, for example, do not include fatalities among employees in the maritime industry, and those arising from the supply or use of flammable gas, and work-related road transport accidents – which almost certainly more than double the above fatality figure, primarily due to the scale of the latter[37]. In addition, non-fatal accident statistics exclude accidents resulting in absences of three days or less, and are known anyway to grossly underestimate the "official" situation because of the failure of employers to report accidents that are legally notifiable by them under the Reporting of Injuries, Diseases and Dangerous Occurrences Regulations. For example, Labour Force Survey (LFS) data for 1996/97 suggests that just under around 60% of reportable accidents involving employees were not actually notified to the relevant enforcement authorities[38].

LFS data further suggests that over a million employed people suffered a non-fatal work-related injury in the year 1996/97[39]. This statistic is worrying enough. It nevertheless provides only a very partial indication of the scale of the harm arising from work activities since, by definition, no account is taken of the work-related illnesses suffered by workers.

No reliable and comprehensive figures exist on the number of deaths occurring each year as a result of work-related illnesses. However, the number of such deaths is known to be extremely large. The HSE has, for example, estimated that at least 3,000 deaths occurr annually as a result of asbestos-related disease alone, and it has been estimated, more generally, that around 20,000 people die each year from work-related medical conditions[40]. Many of these deaths of course stem from exposure to harmful substances which happened many years ago. At the same time care must be taken not to underestimate either the number of deaths that are likely to occur as a result of current exposure to workplace risks or the extent to which workers, more generally, suffer work-related illnesses. Thus, HSE commissioned research, which sought information from households covered by the 1995 LFS, reveals that at least two million people considered themselves to have suffered from an illness that had been caused, or made worse, by work during the year[41]. The most commonly reported of these illnesses being musculoskeletal disorders (1.2 million), stress, depression and anxiety (279,000), other stress-ascribed diseases (254,000), lower respiratory disease (202,000) and deafness, tinnitus or other ear conditions (170,000).

These figures clearly illustrate, yet again, how often workers have to put their health and safety at risk to earn a living. Those relating to musculoskeletal disorders and stress further suggest that there is an urgent need to encourage employers to not only pay much greater attention to the protection of workers from "traditional" health risks, such as occupational deafness, but to adopt a more holistic approach to the management of occupational health which encompasses a consideration of how workers' health is affected by management decisions relating to the length and distribution of working time, the design of work tasks and worker-customer interactions. Moreover, the need for such an approach is further supported by findings from HSE supported household surveys which sought information on the working conditions experienced by workers. For example, these show that around 20% of workers considered that they always/nearly always had too much work to do, 32% always/nearly always had to repeat the same sequence of movements many times in their job, and 13% always/nearly always worked in awkward or tiring positions[42].

The way forward

SELF-REGULATION as advocated by the Robens Committee and prescribed in HS(G)65 appears, at least in theory, to provide a firm basis for advancing health and safety standards. In practice, however, there appears no doubt that many, if not most, organisations neither have the willingness or capacity to develop management systems that embody the alleged virtues of self-regulation. That they do not is borne out by existing research evidence and the results of public enquiries. It is also demonstrated by the massive scale of harm suffered by workers, both in the form of workplace injuries and work-related ill health.

In advancing a self-regulatory approach the Robens Committee in effect took the view that employers could be persuaded to effectively manage health and safety. This same theme has continued to be pursued by the HSE through a variety of publications and guidance. The evidence reviewed in this chapter, and summarised in the preceding paragraph, suggests that such a viewpoint is to say the least optimistic – not withstanding the strenuous efforts made by some employers to reduce workforce accidents and ill health. Consequently, there seems no doubt that the Robens Committee underestimated the degree to which the behaviour of employers needed to be legally regulated.

In subsequent chapters attention is paid to the related issues of legal enforcement, worker representation and the amelioration of work-related harm. In each of these a variety of proposals are put forward to improve the present situation in the area concerned. Many of these proposals are primarily aimed at putting mechanisms in place to encourage employers to accord health and safety a greater priority and to manage it more effectively. However, in themselves they are unlikely to be sufficient unless action is also taken to both clarify and strengthen the legal duties imposed on employers.

In our view this action needs to embody the following, and inevitably, inter-related elements:

- the major reform of the general duties laid down under sections 2 and 3 of the HSW Act;
- the creation of a statutory framework on occupational health and safety services; and
- the adoption of an approach to the drafting of regulations and supporting ACOPs which places greater emphasis on prescriptive requirements and guidance.

Reform of the general duties

At present the general duties imposed under sections 2 and 3 are vague to the point of opacity with the result that they fail to provide a clear statutory outline of what employers need to do to manage health and safety effectively. In addition, the qualification of them in terms of reasonable practicability is not only legally questionable, given the provisions of the EC framework directive, but also overly generous, particularly if the business case for investing in health and safety advanced by both the HSE and government is valid.

The generality of sections 2 and 3 is admittedly mitigated by provisions laid down in supporting regulations, notably the MHSW Regulations. However, these regulations do not go so far as to lay down a "model" which details all of the elements which HS(G)65 argues are central to the effective management of health and safety. Moreover, insofar as they do, it is surely strange that such statutory guidance is not embodied in the HSW Act itself.

Consequently, there seems a strong case for the general duties in the Act to not only lay down goal-orientated objectives, but also specify in broad terms the "organisation and arrangements", to paraphrase the health and safety policy requirements of section 2(3), that employers need to put in place and the principles that should inform their development. Obviously there is scope for much debate as to how these provisions should be drafted. However, the end result should be that employers are left in no doubt that they need to assess risks to both employees and non-employees; clearly outline health and safety responsibilities; provide adequate information, instruction and training, prioritise the removal of risk as a means of protection, adapt work schedules and patterns to the abilities and capabilities, both physical and mental, of workers; investigate accidents and cases of occupational ill health; and regularly monitor and evaluate health and safety performance.

This broad specification of employer health and safety organisation and arrangements could be supplemented by more detailed regulations or guidance where necessary. For example, further guidance on them could be provided in an ACOP that contained details of the steps that should be taken in respect of such matters as the auditing and measurement of health and safety performance, the planning and organisation of induction training, the allocation of management responsibilities, and the obtaining and utilisation of information from suppliers of articles and substances. In light of the earlier analysis, there would also seem a case for supplementing them with new regulations covering such matters as the management of road transport risks, the ergonomic design of work tasks and schedules, and temporary working and sub-contracting. These last regulations could, in turn, contain, or be supported by, requirements which oblige government departments, other public bodies and large companies to engage in 'contract compliance' – that is to establish mechanisms through which contracts are only awarded to organisations that can demonstrate good health and safety standards.

As regards the use of the phrase reasonably practicable, we propose that this should be removed and replaced by one that requires employer actions to protect workers to be evaluated in terms of their adequacy rather than their costs and benefits. It is, however, a moot point whether this would be sufficient to bring British law into line with European requirements.

Occupational health and safety services

The evidence reviewed earlier indicates that in most workplaces there is no access to either safety specialists or occupational health specialists. It further indicates that where the latter do exist, they frequently play a relatively limited role with regard to the identification and prevention of occupational ill health.

A major contributor to this situation is undoubtedly the fact that for the most part current law does no more than require employers to appoint one or more "competent persons" to assist them in undertaking measures to comply with their statutory duties – an approach which, as previously noted, is likely to breach the requirements of the EC framework directive. As a result employers are accorded considerable discretion in terms of the use made of preventive health and safety services. This situation therefore differs considerably to that which exists in most EU member states, where legislative requirements are laid down in respect of the use and composition of such services, including the qualifications and skills to be possessed by those employed within them.

For both legal and practical reasons there seems a strong case for adopting a statutory framework under which all employers would be required to have access, either internally or through accreditated external providers, to occupational health and safety services of a specified quality. This framework should specify the skills which must be available within such services, the tasks which they are required to carry out and the level of service that they must provide, perhaps in terms of hours per employee. It is, however, recognised that their may be a need to vary the requirements imposed to reflect the differing needs of particular industry sectors.

Once again there would clearly need to be a lengthy process of debate about the precise framing of the above framework, as well as the action needed to ensure an adequate supply of appropriately qualified staff. Nevertheless, in our view, the framework developed should embody two fundamental features. First, a recognition that the staff skills needed extend beyond safety specialists, and occupational doctors and nurses to encompass other types of professionals, such as ergonomists, physiotherapists and occupational psychologists. In other words a recognition of the fact that the multi-factorial nature of many current health and safety problems necessitates, in turn, the adoption of a multi-disciplinary (and holistic) approach to its management. That is, one which not only addresses "hardware" and "software" issues, but also the inter-relationships that occur between them. Secondly, an acceptance that the services to be provided must be jointly controlled in order to ensure that they operate in an independent way and are not dominated by employer views and interests.

More prescriptive regulation

In calling for greater prescription we are not arguing, as the above discussion of the general duties laid down under sections 2 and 3 of the HSW Act makes clear, for a complete move back to the pre-Robens approach to the drafting of statutory requirements. Rather what we are arguing is that the shift towards goal-orientated duties has at times gone too far and at times been used to provide employers with unnecessary and, at least in the case of SMEs, confusing discretion. A simple illustration of this is the way in which the Workplace (Health, Safety and Welfare) Regulations merely require employers to provide a reasonable workplace temperature, while their supporting ACOP refrains from providing any guidance on the level at which working temperatures become unacceptably high[43].

Numerous other examples can be given of similar situations where overly general regulatory duties are supported by almost equally general supporting ACOP guidance. A good case in point concerns the requirements laid down on the appointment of competent persons under the Management of Health and Safety at Work Regulations. Thus, not only do these regulations, as noted earlier, define such persons, in almost tautological terms, as one who "has sufficient training and experience or knowledge and other qualities to enable him properly to assist..." but their supporting code merely observes that: "Competence in the sense it is used in these Regulations does not necessarily depend on the possession of particular skills or qualifications. Simple situations may require only (a) an understanding of relevant current best practice; (b) an understanding of the limitations of one's own experience and knowledge and (c) the willingness and ability to supplement existing experience and knowledge...".

Indeed, and more generally, all too often ACOPs fall far short of providing the "practical guidance" that the Robens Committee argued they should. One reason for this would appear to be that, except where they support industry-specific regulations, they are drafted to apply to all types of work situation. Insofar as this is the case, there would consequently seem a case, as the Robens Committee recommended, for placing greater reliance on the development of sectoral-based codes which provide clearer and more comprehensible guidance to their readers. The issue of how a move in this direction could be supported is one to which we return in chapter 5.

Conclusion

THE self-regulatory framework laid down under the HSW Act, by according greater importance to management organisation and processes, represented an advance on the previously existing statutory system for occupational health and safety. However, the evidence reviewed in this chapter raises major concerns about its effectiveness. For it reveals that the scale of work-related harm suffered by workers remains enormous. It also indicates that many employers neither have the willingness or capacity to management health and safety effectively, particularly against a background of recent trends towards the use of more devolved management structures and the greater utilisation of more distant and transitory employment relationships.

A number of proposals have been put forward to address these related problems and hence improve the current statutory framework. These focus attention on three main issues. First, the reform of the general duties imposed under sections 2 and 3 of the HSW Act, most notably through a more detailed specification of the health and safety organisation and arrangements that employers need to put in place. Secondly, the introduction of a statutory framework under which all employers would be required to have access to multi-disciplinary occupational health and safety services. Thirdly, the greater use of prescriptive regulatory requirements and guidance along with the placing of more emphasis on sectoral-based regulations and/or ACOPs.

Summary of key points

Employers and their legal duties

- amendment of the general duties laid down under sections 2 and 3 of the HSW Act so that they specify in broad terms the management "organisation and arrangements" that employers need to put in place in respect of the management of health and safety at work, as well as the preventive principles that should inform their development;
- removal of the qualification of the above duties in terms of reasonable practicability and its replacement by one that requires employer actions to be evaluated in terms of their adequacy;
- the introduction of an Approved Code of Practice (ACOP) to provide detailed guidance on these revised duties;
- making of new regulations on the management of road transport risks, temporary working and sub-contracting, and the ergonomic design of work tasks and schedules;
- creation of a statutory framework under which all employers would be required to have access, either internally or through accredited external providers, to occupational health and safety services of a specified quality;
- the placing of these services under the joint control of employer and worker representatives;
- reduction in the reliance placed on goal-orientated regulatory duties; and
- the increased use of sectoral-specific regulations and ACOPs.

Notes

1 *Lord Robens, Safety and Health at Work: Report of the Committee* 1970-72, Cmnd 5034, HMSO, 1972, para 45.
2 P. James, "Occupational Health and Safety: The Impact of the Single European Act", *Review of Employment Topics*, 3(1), 1995.
3 The Management of Health and Safety at Work Regulations 1992 (SI 1992 No. 2051).
4 *Successful Health and Safety Management*, HS(G)65(revised), HSE Books, 1997.
5 For a discussion of this distinction between "willingness" and "capacity" see S. Dawson, P. Willman, M. Bamford and A. Clinton, *"Safety at Work: The Limits of Self Regulation"*, Cambridge University Press, 1988.
6 See *Edwards v National Coal Board* [1949] 1 K.B.704.
7 Health and Safety Executive, *"The Costs of Accidents at Work"*, HS(G)96, HMSO.
8 T. Cutler and P. James, "Does Safety Pay? A Critical Account of the Health and Safety Executive Document: The Costs of Accidents", *Work, Employment and Society*, 10, 1996, 755-765.
9 Department of Transport, *Merchant Shipping Act 1984: MV Herald of Free Enterprise*, 1987, HMSO.
10 Department of Energy, *"The Public Inquiry into the Piper Alpha Disaster"*, HMSO, 1990.
11 Department of Transport, *"Investigation into the Clapham Junction Railway Accident"*, HMSO, 1989.
12 J. Wrench and G. Lee, "Piecework and Industrial Accidents: Two Contemporary Case Studies", *Sociology*, 16(1), 1982.
13 See eg. T. Nichols, "Labour Intensification, Work Injuries and the Measurement of the Percentage Utilisation of Labour", *British Journal of Industrial Relations*, 29(4); L. Grunberg, "Workplace Relations in the Economic Crises: A Comparison of a British and a French Automobile Plant", *Sociology*, 20(4); and C. Woolfson, J. Foster and M. Beck, *"Paying the Piper: Capital and Labour in Britain's Offshore Oil Industry"*, Mansell, 1996.
14 A. Smith, S. Johal, E. Wadsworth, I. Harvey, G. Smith and T. Peters, "Stress and Health at Work, Part IV", *Occupational Health Review*, 80, July/August 1999, 28-31.
15 C. Baldry, P. Bain and P. Taylor, "Sick and Tired? - Working in the Modern Office", *Work, Employment and Society*, 11(3), 519-539.
16 J. Osborne and M. Zairi, *"Total Quality Management and the Management of Health and Safety"*, Contract Research Report 153/1997, Health and Safety Executive.
17 M. Hanson, K. Tesh, S. Groat, P. Donnan, P. Ritchie and R. Lancaster, *"Evaluation of the Six-Pack Regulations 1992"*, Contract Research Report 177/1998, Health and Safety Executive.
18 "Dark ages safety practices kill worker and put Sainsbury's in the fine record book", *Health and Safety Bulletin*, 274, December 1998, 2.
19 D. Walters (ed), *"Occupational Health and Safety Strategies in Europe, Vol 1 The National Situations"*, European Foundation for the Improvement of Living and Working Conditions, 1996, Office for Official Publications of the European Communities.

20 K. Bunt, *"Occupational Health Provision at Work"*, Contract Research Report 57/1993, Health and Safety Executive.

21 *"Revitalising Health and Safety"*, HSC/DETR Consultation Document, July 1999.

22 *"Small and Large Manufacturing Workplaces: Rates of Workplace Injury"* 1994/95-1995/96, Health and Safety Executive Factsheet, 1998. Also see T. Nichols, *"The Sociology of Industrial Injury"*, Mansell, 1997, chapter 7.

23 Health and Safety Commission, *"Review of Health and Safety Regulation"*, 1994, HSE Books.

24 Health and Safety Executive, *"Improving Compliance with Safety Procedures: Reducing Industrial Violations"*, 1995, HSE Books.

25 See eg. *"Human Factors in Industrial Safety"*, HS(G)48, HMSO, 1989.

26 See eg. L. Harris and E. Ogbonna, "Employee Responses to Culture Change Efforts", *Human Resource Management Journal,* 8(2), 1998, 78-92.

27 For a general overview of these developments see D. Walters and P. James, *"Robens Revisited: The Case for a Review of Occupational Health and Safety Legislation"*, 1998, Institute of Employment Rights.

28 A. Felstead, N. Jewson and J. Goodwin, *"Homeworkers in Britain"*, HMSO.

29 *"Revitalising Health and Safety"*, op cit.

30 C. James, "Self-employed and Employee Transport Workers: Labour Process Determinants of Occupational Injury", *Labour and Industry,* 5(3), 1993, 75-90; and C. Mayhew and M. Quinlan, "Subcontracting and Occupational Health and safety in the Residential Building Industry", *Industrial Relations Journal,* 28(3), 1997, 192-205.

31 European Foundation for the Improvement of Living and Working Conditions, Second European Survey of the Working Environment, 1997, Office for Official Publications of the European Communities.

32 *"Revitalising Health and Safety"*, op cit.

33 See *"Health and Safety Commission, Annual Report 1994/95"*, 1995, HSE Books; and *"Revitalising Health and Safety"*, op cit. Also see S. Tombs, "Injury, Death and the Deregulation Fetish: The Politics of Occupational Safety Regulation in UK Manufacturing Industries", *International Journal of Health Services,* 26(2), 1996, 309-329.

34 Nichols, 1997, op cit.

35 *"Revitalising Health and Safety"*, op cit, page 6.

36 Ibid.

37 see S. Tombs, *"Another Week, Another Piper? Death and Work in Britain"*, paper presented at the Piper Alpha Tenth Anniversary Conference, 3 July 1998, University of Glasgow.

38 Health and Safety Commission, *"Health and Safety Statistics 1997/98"*, 1998, HSE Books.

39 Ibid.

40 See respectively *"Revitalising Health and Safety"*, op cit; and GMB, *"Hazards at Work: GMB Proposals for Reducing Risks to Workers and the Public"*, 1987, GMB.

41 JR Jones, JT Hodgson, TA Clegg and RC Elliott, *"Self-reported Work-related Illness in 1995: Results from a Household Survey"*, 1998, HSE Books.

42 Ibid.

43 *"Workplace (Health, Safety and Welfare) Regulations"* 1992 (SI 1992 No.3004).

Chapter 3

The administration of the statutory framework

HISTORICAL analyses show that the operation of market forces does not guarantee the presence of adequate standards of health and safety. Indeed the available evidence indicates only too clearly that such forces, when linked to employer freedom to determine the actions to be taken to protect workers, are likely to result in health and safety issues being accorded an unacceptably low priority[1]. In fact it was precisely this feature of their operation that led to the introduction of legislation to regulate the actions of employers in respect of occupational health and safety[2].

Protective health and safety legislation is therefore necessary if workers are not to suffer unacceptable levels of injury and ill health as a result of their work. Its mere presence is not, however, sufficient. This is for two reasons. First, the requirements laid down may be inadequate – as the discussion of self-regulation by employers in chapter 2 demonstrates. Secondly, those on whom they are imposed may not comply with them. In combination these two factors therefore highlight the fact that the evaluation of any statutory system of health and safety law requires attention to be paid to the way in which its provisions are developed and enforced. In short, how the system is administered.

In Britain this process of administration is carried out by three main sets of actors – the Health and Safety Commission (HSC), the Health and Safety Executive (HSE) and Environmental Health Officers (EHOs) employed by local authorities. Consequently, this chapter examines the roles, resources and activities of these actors. More specifically, the chapter initially outlines their statutory responsibilities and the way in which they are organised to carry them out. This outline is then followed by a critical examination of the resources at their disposal and the way in which these are used. Finally, a concluding section puts forward a variety of proposals aimed at improving the way in which the present statutory framework is administered.

The administrative system

THE HSC was established under the HSW Act and is required to consist of a Chair and between six and nine other members. In filling six of these positions, the government must consult with organisations representing "employers" for three of the them and those representing "employees" to fill the other three. In order to fill the remaining seats – which are not mandatory – the government must consult "such organisations, including professional bodies, the activities of whose members are concerned with matters" relating to the purposes of the Act. At present, these three seats comprise two members representing a "local authority" background and one representing a "consumer" background.

The statutory functions of the Commission encompass assisting and encouraging persons to further the general purposes of the Act; making arrangements for the carrying out of research and the publication of its results; providing an information and advisory service to those concerned with matters relevant to the objectives of the Act; and submitting proposals for regulations. Various powers are given to the Commission, including rights relating to the ordering of investigations and inquiries and the approval, with the consent of the Secretary of State, of ACOPs. More generally, the Commission is required to give effect to any directions given to it by the Secretary of State, including directions modifying its functions.

In carrying out its work the HSC draws on advice from 25 advisory committees, boards and councils. Some of these deal with particular hazard areas and others with particular industries. For example, advisory committees exist in respect of genetic modification, toxic subjects, nuclear installations and the construction, foundries and textile industries. Each of the bodies consist of people nominated by employer and employee organisations. In addition, they often include "public interest representatives" and technological and professional experts.

The HSE acts as the operational arm of the Commission. It is required "to make adequate arrangements for the enforcement of the relevant statutory provisions" and more generally, to comply with any directions given to it by the latter in pursuance of its functions. However, the Commission is specifically forbidden from instructing the Executive as to how it enforces the statutory provisions in any particular case.

On its establishment the HSE brought together the existing factory, agricultural, quarry, mining and other inspectorates, together with their research and technology functions. Subsequently, it also became the home for the offshore and railway inspectorates (see chapter 1). The fieldwork undertaken by HSE inspectors is, however, "paralleled" by local authority EHOs whose areas of enforcement responsibility generally cover "lower" risk areas of activity, such as retailing, leisure, and hotels and catering[3]. Although outside the HSC structure, EHOs are required to "perform their duty... in accordance with such guidance as the [Health and Safety] Commission may give them". An HSE/local authority liaison committee (HELA) exists to provide liaison between HSE and local authorities, and in particular, to ensure that a consistent approach is adopted towards enforcement.

The HSE's work covers three main areas: the carrying out of inspections and other regulatory activity to secure legal compliance; policy formulation, including the development of new legislation and ACOPs; and "science and technology" – a term that encompasses both the carrying out and commissioning of research and the provision of scientific and technological advice. However, its activities also encompass the provision of information and advice about the hazards and risks of work activities to employers, workers and members of the public, and the assessing, approval and certification of particular products and substances under various statutory schemes. The table below details the proportion of staff time and costs expended on each of these areas of activities

Distribution of HSE staff time and costs by type of activity

Type of activity	% staff time	% staff costs
Developing policy and proposing legislation	16	19
Inspection and other regulatory activity to secure legal compliance	51	52
Provision of information and advice	8.7	8.5
Statutory assessments, approvals and certification	3.8	3.5
Promotion of risk assessment and technological knowledge	9.5	9.8
Central services	10.6	7.5

Source: Health and Safety Commission Annual Report and Accounts 1997/98, 1998, HSE Books

The above figures are relatively self-explanatory. However, it should be noted that "inspection and other regulatory activities" not only encompass preventive inspections and the investigation of accidents and complaints, but also a number of other types of activity. For example, advisory visits, visits in connection with the issuing of enforcement notices or court attendances, National Interest Group work and workplace contact officer "involvement" with low hazard/ low risk workplaces. It should further be borne in mind that these last two types of activity do not for the most part involve any workplace visits.

On 1 April 1998 the HSE employed 3,932 staff. Of these, 1,437 were inspectors, although a proportion of them were engaged on non-inspection duties and hence were not directly engaged in activities to secure compliance in the more than 600,000 premises for which the HSE is responsible. For their part local authorities employed the equivalent of 1,440 full-time EHOs to carry out enforcement activities in the around 1,210,000 establishments falling within their jurisdiction.

Operation of the administrative system

BELOW we explore the operation of the present system for administering the statutory framework for occupational health and safety through a consideration of seven issues. These are: the setting of regulatory standards; the use of inspections and investigations by inspectors; the enforcement action taken by them; the penalties imposed following successful prosecutions; the enforcement arrangements that exist in respect of occupational health; and the role of corporate manslaughter charges.

1. Setting of regulatory standards

The HSC, in developing proposals for new (and revised) regulations and ACOPs, draws on the expertise of its advisory bodies and informal consultations with relevant organisations. In some cases, discussion documents may also be issued to gather views on the desirability of regulations and the form that they should take. Once formulated, draft regulations and ACOPs are published for public consultation. The results of this consultation are then analysed and, where it is deemed necessary, amendments made to the draft proposals. They are then submitted for approval. First, by the Commission itself, then by the Secretary of State and finally by Parliament.

In recent years many of the regulations made through the above process have been developed in order to bring domestic law into line with the requirements of European directives (see chapter 1). A noteworthy feature of this transposition process, and indeed HSC regulation drafting more generally, has been an attempt on the part of the Commission to continue to place reliance as far as possible on the laying down of goal-orientated duties of the type recommended by the Robens Committee. This approach has at times, because of the more prescriptive nature of many European requirements, led to them being transposed in an inadequate and questionable way[4]. It has also, as discussed in chapter 2, created problems for smaller employers in terms of understanding what they need to do to comply with their legal duties. Moreover, as also highlighted in chapter 2, these problems have frequently not been adequately resolved through the guidance provided in supporting ACOPs.

In effect therefore it would seem that in drafting regulatory proposals (and associated ACOPs) the HSC adopts an approach that better meets the needs of larger, often unionised, employers. This, in turn, suggests that it is the wishes of such employers that tend to exert most influence over the HSC decision-making process.

2. HSE inspections and investigations

Both HSE and local authority inspectors undertake "preventative inspections" and "investigations" into reported incidents and complaints. These inspections and investigations in fact form the bulk of the work undertaken by inspectors in order to secure legal compliance. For example, inspections constitute around 56% of all "regulatory contacts" and investigations take up 18%[5].

Inspections. In 1997/98 HSE inspectors made 104,000 and EHO 215,000 visits. In theory these figures suggest that in both sectors, every workplace should, on average, receive a visit every 5 or 6 years. However, in practice both sets of inspectors target those workplaces which are considered high risk. As a result, some workplaces will be visited many times during a six year period, whilst others – deemed low risk – may not receive an inspection at all over that period.

In pursuing this "focused" inspection strategy, HSE inspectors have in recent years periodically undertaken "blitzes" in such hazardous industries as construction and agriculture. For example, last year, in a series of two-week inspection blitzes, 122 inspectors made 4,500 visits to farms and further such blitzes have been undertaken this year. More generally, the HSE's Field Operations Directorate (FOD) focuses much of its inspection efforts on small firms. Thus, 81% of the planned inspections undertaken by its staff last year were conducted in such companies.

At the same time, FOD has been placing greater emphasis on carrying out more in-depth audits of management systems in large organisations, particularly those that have high-hazard sites. This shift of approach, in turn, appears to have resulted in a decline in the number of inspections undertaken per staff year[6].

Investigations. Employers are legally obliged to report to the HSE a number of different types of incident: "over three day injuries", "major injuries, and fatalities, and certain dangerous occurrences and occupational diseases[7]. However, as noted in chapter 2, less than half of all notifiable injuries are actually so reported.

It appears that all sudden workplace deaths – over 3,000 in the last 10 years – are reported to the HSE and are subsequently investigated. However, the HSE only investigates 7% of all accidents reported to it, including just 12% of those causing major injuries. In considering which major injuries to investigate, an inspector considers:

- the actual and potential severity of the event;
- the seriousness of any potential breach of the law;
- the track record of the duty holder;
- enforcement priorities, both national and local;
- the practicality of achieving results; and
- the relevance of the event to a wider range of premises[8].

Despite these criteria, even amongst the most serious of the major injuries, a high percentage remain uninvestigated. For example, 60% of burns and 58% of amputations[9]. In addition, there is a high level of variation in the investigation rates of HSE area offices around the country. So, for example, whilst the Home Counties investigated 62% of amputations in the last two years, London and the South East investigated only 33%.

3. Enforcement action

Inspectors, as explained in chapter 1, can issue improvement and prohibition notices: the former being servable where it is believed that a person is contravening one or more relevant statutory provisions, and the latter where it is believed that activities are being (or are about to be) carried out which involve a risk of serious personal injury. Improvement notices give the person on whom they are served a period within which to remedy the contravention, this period being no less than 21 days. Prohibition notices can take effect on an immediate or deferred basis.

In addition, inspectors can initiate prosecutions. Section 33 of the HSW Act details 15 different types of offences that can give rise to prosecution. These fall into two categories: those triable summarily before a magistrates court and those triable either summarily or on indictment before a Crown Court. The latter category covers such offences as a failure to comply with an improvement or prohibition notice, and a failure to discharge any duties imposed under sections 2-9 of the HSW Act. Where an offence committed by a body corporate is proved to have been committed with the consent or connivance of, of have been attributable to any neglect, on the part of any director, manager secretary or other similar officer, that person can also, by virtue of section 37(1) of the HSW Act, be prosecuted.

The maximum penalty applicable to a person found guilty on summary conviction varies by type of offence. Thus, breaches of the forgoing general duties, as well as failures to comply with enforcement notices, can give rise to a £20,000 fine, other breaches to a £5,000 fine. The failure to comply with an enforcement notice can also result in a prison sentence of up to six months. In the case of convictions on indictment, no limit is placed on the fine and those guilty of certain offences can be imprisoned for up to two years. In addition, both magistrate and Crown Courts have the power, under section 42 of the HSW Act, to make an order requiring a convicted person to "remedy the cause of the offence".

Use of notices. HSE inspectors issued 8,812 enforcement notices during 1997/98 – over half of which were prohibition notices. If this total is compared with the number of inspections and investigations undertaken, then it appears that one notice is issued per 15.77 such visits – a ratio that translates into the issuing of 63 notices per 1,000 inspections and investigations. This, however, is an over-estimate since some inspections result in more than one notice being served.

For their part, EHOs issued 4,510 formal notices in 1997/8, nearly three-quarters of these were improvement notices. As a result, on average, nine improvement notices and three prohibition notices were issued per 1,000 visits. These averages, however, conceal marked variations in the rates applying to different types of authority. For example, the rate for improvement notice usage ranged from 17 per 1,000 visits in Metropolitan authorities to 4 per 1,000 for Scottish rural authorities.

Prosecutions. The HSE prosecuted a total of 1,654 offences, involving 952 "duty holders", in 1997/98, of which 77% resulted in conviction. This is a 10% increase in the number of informations laid compared to the previous year – though there has been a general downward trend in the number of prosecutions; 10 years earlier in 1987/88, the HSE prosecuted 30% more cases – a total of 2,337 offences.

The relationship between HSE inspections and prosecutions is not easily identified. First, because one inspection may lead to a company being prosecuted for a number of offences. Secondly, because a significant proportion of these prosecutions – about 20% – will have followed investigations into death or injury rather than inspection[10]. However, if we generously ignore the latter fact and therefore assume that all 952 prosecutions of duty holders arose from inspections, then this suggests that at best one inspection in 109 led to a prosecution.

As regards prosecutions brought by local authority inspectors, the latest figures show that 506 informations were laid in 1997/98 and 87% of these resulted in a conviction. It appears that, on average, less than one visit in every 200 gave rise to a prosecution.

The level of prosecution after major injury and death is also low. Nevertheless, there is a higher level of prosecutions following injury investigations compared to inspections[11]. Thus, between 1996-98, 10% of all the major injuries and 23% of the deaths investigated resulted in prosecutions – notwithstanding the HSE's own conclusion that around 70% of all workplace deaths are the result of "management failure". At the same time there is a high level of variation in different parts of the country. For example, while 10% of investigated burns in Wales and the West resulted in prosecution, only 2% of those investigated in the Home Counties resulted in such legal action.

Two other important points about this prosecution activity should also be highlighted. The first is that the overwhelming majority of prosecutions concern corporate entities rather than individuals. For example, out of the 1,654 offences prosecuted by the HSE last year, only six concerned senior company officers. This compares to 24 related to individual workers. Secondly, the vast bulk of prosecutions are brought before magistrates courts rather than taken on indictment.

This is also true of most of the prosecutions taken following a death and major injury. In fact all the prosecutions taken between 1996-98 in respect of workplace deaths in two of HSE's regions (the Midlands and the North West) were prosecuted in this way. Interestingly, however, in the North East region during the same period, 30% of such prosecutions were taken on indictment before a Crown Court. Strikingly, these resulted in much higher fines than those in the Midlands and North West – £17,300 compared with £6,000

4. Penalties following convictions

The average fine for each conviction secured during 1997/98 by the HSE was £4,785, a figure which is almost seven times higher than the corresponding figure for 10 years earlier. This average fine, however, includes those prosecutions which relate to death and injury – which gain a generally higher sentence – so the average fine following a prosecution arising from an inspection is far lower. Indeed, if fines of over £100,000 are excluded, the overall average falls to £3,886. This figure compares with an average fine of £2,224 imposed following a successful local authority prosecution.

On 6 November 1998, the Court of Appeal gave some guidance to courts in sentencing companies convicted of health and safety offences[12]. In particular, the Court stated that in assessing the gravity of a breach attention should be paid to:

- "...how far short of the appropriate standard the defendant fell in failing to meet the reasonably practicable test." and
- the "degree of risk and extent of the danger created by the offence," and
- the defendant's resources and the effect of the fine on its business

In addition, the Court identified the following aggravating factors that should be taken into account when applying the above principles:

- a resulting death: "Generally where death is the consequence of a criminal act it is regarded as an aggravating feature of the offence."
- a "deliberate breach of the health and safety legislation with a view to profit"; and
- a "failure to heed warnings."

There are signs that this guidance may be encouraging courts to impose higher fines. Certainly the taking into account of the "defendant's resources and the effect of the fine on its business" could address the fact that, until now, fines are rarely influenced by company profits or turnover. For example, the West Midlands Health and Safety Advice Centre obtained information on the annual profits of 65 of the 260 companies sentenced in the region between 1987 and 1993. An analysis of this revealed that the five companies with average profits of between £1-10,000 received an average fine of £750 per offence, which amounted to 16% of their profits; companies with profits of between £100-150,000 received fines of £1,290 per offence, amounting to 0.5% of their profits; and the five companies with profits of over £10 million received average fines of £1,185, equivalent to 0.002% of their profits[13].

No court has so far imposed an order on an employer under section 42 of the HSW Act to "remedy the cause of the offence". Indeed, as far as anyone knows, no HSE inspector has ever suggested to a court that such an order should be made. Recent years have, however, seen a number of prison sentences imposed on individual managers, although virtually all these have stemmed from manslaughter charges laid against the directors of small companies[14].

5. Enforcement and health: the Employment Medical Advisory Service

The link between work and ill-health (rather than work and safety) is often difficult to prove but it is beyond doubt that cases of work related ill-health outweigh sudden deaths and injuries by a factor of at least ten (see chapter 2). EHO and HSE inspectors are supposed to enforce health standards along with their work on safety. They are however assisted by the Employment Medical Advisory Service (EMAS).

EMAS was first established in 1972, and its existence was continued by section 55 of the HSW Act. When EMAS first started, most of its work centred on conducting medical surveillance of workers as well as supporting, advising and encouraging health professionals in the field of occupational health. To this end, Employment Medical Advisors (EMAs) were empowered to medically examine workers (without the consent of the employers) when they considered that their work was damaging to health and were also given powers to enter premises, carry out inspections and obtain documents and other relevant information from employers.

It was originally intended that EMAS would employ 120 doctors along with nursing and support staff. They have never employed this level of doctors; in 1978, at its height, for example, there were only 86 doctors (along with 85 nurses). Since then, the numbers of staff have been steadily declining to the point where the service now employs only 23 doctors and 22 nurses.

There have been recent changes in EMAS. First, the EMAs have now become Medical Inspectors, and Employment Nursing Advisors are now HMI of Health and Safety (Occupational Health). Secondly, they have been given powers to impose enforcement notices and all EMAS staff are given more training in general inspection and enforcement techniques. However, according to the new director of EMAS, it is not envisaged that her staff will normally need to use their enforcement powers, as decisions on enforcement will continue to be a matter for the inspector responsible for day-to-day inspection of premises. As a result the specialist expertise of EMAs will, unfortunately, continue to only indirectly influence HSE enforcement action.

6. The issue of manslaughter

HSE inspectors only have jurisdiction over health and safety offences; they have no responsibility to conduct investigations into other crimes that may have been committed, like that of manslaughter. However, this offence – which requires evidence of gross negligence – may well have been committed (in relation to a workplace death) by a director or senior company officer.

HSE's policy toward manslaughter has changed in the last ten years. In 1989, John Rimington, the then Director General of the HSE wrote, in an article about corporate accountability, that:

"[HSE inspectors] receive thorough training in all aspects of criminal law which they need for their work including guidance on when to refer a case to the police. Discussions between the HSE inspectors and police or the Crown Prosecution Service will take place if the most appropriate charge is one not available to an HSE Inspector[15]."

Yet, at the time, this was not true. Though, in 1986, inspectors did receive guidance on relations between them and the police and the Crown Prosecution Service, it did not concern corporate manslaughter. It only related to a situation where a worker died or was injured as a result of worker "skylarking" or dangerous driving[16].

However by 1993, change was in the air. The HSE had provided its inspectors with new guidance on when to refer a possible case of corporate manslaughter to the police. This guidance states:

"Evidence which points towards a manslaughter charge should be referred to the police. They will decide whether the evidence warrants referral to the CPS. A copy of all the papers sent to the police should be sent to the HSE Solicitors office. HSE's solicitor will consider the papers and if the evidence appears sufficiently strong may refer the case directly to the CPS and inform the police accordingly.[17]"

Since this guidance has been produced, the HSE has referred 56 (out of over 1,600 workplace deaths) to the police or Crown Prosecution Service[18]. However, only 24 of these referrals related to potential manslaughter on the part of directors or senior managers. Of these, three have led to a subsequent conviction – one relating to a workplace death and two others to the deaths of members of the public.

These official figures contrast with the results of independent studies. In 1994, the West Midlands Health and Safety Advice Centre reinvestigated 24 deaths that took place in the region between 1988 and 1992. On the basis of this new evidence, Anthony Scrivener QC stated that four of the deaths should have resulted in a

---

manslaughter prosecution against a director. If this was reflected nation-wide, last years deaths alone should have resulted in 45 corporate manslaughter prosecutions[13]. New research, published at the beginning of the year, moreover, supports Scrivener's assessment by concluding that 20% of the 28 deaths examined should have been referred to the Crown Prosecution Service for consideration as to the bringing of corporate manslaughter charges[19].

In May 1998, the HSE, CPS and the Association of Chief Police Officers (ACPO) published a new protocol of liaison on workplace death. This gives the police a formal investigative role; from now on, a police detective of supervisory rank will attend the scene of every workplace death and make an initial assessment about whether "the circumstances might justify a charge of manslaughter." The protocol further provides that the police will investigate "where there is evidence or a suspicion of deliberate intent or gross negligence or recklessness on the part of an individual or company rather than human error or carelessness."

7. Research

In 1998/99 the HSE spent £23 million of its own money on research plus additional sums provided by industry and the European Commission. The bulk of this £23 million was spent on research commissioned via the HSE's Mainstream Research Programme from private industry, consultants, government laboratories, universities and the Health and Safety Laboratory – an in-house agency which competes for contracts on the same basis as external contractors and also provides scientific and technical support to other HSE activities, such as accident enquiries.

Under the current Mainstream programme areas of research interest, both current and future, are detailed under four broad headings: occupational health, major hazards and risk assessment, engineering, and behavioural and social sciences[20]. This programme undoubtedly addresses issues of importance and relevance. The fact nevertheless remains that HSE research funding has fallen in real terms by £5.8 million since 1993/94. This fall in expenditure moreover needs to be considered alongside the more general decline that has occurred nationally in health and safety related research.

Research into occupational health in Britain increased rapidly in the immediate post-war period. This increase resulted in a situation whereby British scientists in the early 1950s became world leaders in subjects such as pneumoconiosis, industrial ergonomics, occupational psychology and occupational cardiovascular disease. Subsequently, however, the scale of occupational health (as well as safety) research declined significantly. In recent years, for example, world renowned centres of research into occupational health and safety have closed and not been replaced. The loss of these centres has moreover been compounded by the closure of a number of industry-based research departments, notably as a result of the privatisation of large, formerly state-owned corporations, such as the National Coal Board. This decline in occupational health research has had adverse consequences for the treatment of some forms of ill health because British specialists continue to argue about points settled decades ago in Scandinavia, North America and Australia. It has also resulted in a situation where those pursuing personal injury claims face, often insurmountable, difficulties as a result of an absence of specialists who can give evidence in support of their case. For example, victims of solvent exposure often have to seek the support of Scandinavian experts because there are no sufficiently qualified expert British witnesses.

The way forward

IN general the creation of the HSC as a central authority for health and safety at work and the establishment of the HSE as its operational arm, has received widespread support. Nevertheless, as the above review has demonstrated, major problems exist with regard to the operation of the present administrative system. Below we therefore put forward a number of proposals for reform. These relate to four main issues: the structure of the HSC, the role of local authority inspectors, enforcement strategies and powers, and HSE resources.

Structure of the HSC

There are undoubted strengths in the basic principles of representation underlying the structure of the HSC and its industry and subject based advisory committees. However, in the light of economic and labour market changes – such as business restructuring, the growth of small enterprises, the change in the balance between core and peripheral labour, as well as the crisis in trade union representation – such structures are in need of review in relation to both their representativeness and their effectiveness.

The creation of these structures some 25 years ago, well in advance of current approaches to public consultation and social dialogue on environmental risk, was facilitated by what was largely a closed system in which the economic interests of employers, the protection of employees and the administration of the state could be expressed through a tripartite system for consultation. At the same time tripartism in health and safety, established at the zenith of the political corporatism of the post-war British state, while being an opportunity for the representatiopn of workers' interests, did little in itself to upset the already established power relations of the scientific/medical/industrial complex. Thus, industry was still able to employ the highest level of professional advice, award the most prestigious research contracts and probably mount the most effective political lobbies to prevent damage to its economic interests[21].

Although the health and safety establishment has tended to view the 1974 Act and the structures it created as a success[22], in fact there is little unqualified empirical evidence of either this success or the possible contribution tripartite consultation may have made towards it. Precisely what progress occurred, and what were its supports and constraints over the last 25 years are consequently unclear. This is unfortunate because such evidence would have been helpful to the development of future strategies. It would be useful to know, for example:

- how far were the system's intentions, as seen from the perspective of the HSE, were implemented in practice[23]. In particular, how much was it possible to separate issues of science from those of economic interest as Locke, the HSE's first Director General, argued would occur through the operation of tripartism?
- what was the nature of the role of expertise in health and safety and what use was made of it by the different interests represented in the tripartite committees? It could be argued for example, that there would be a tendency for the closed structures of tripartism to perpetuate a system in which the vested interests of the powerful were maintained through the accommodation and neutralising of dissent;
- what were the most successful strategies adopted by workers' representatives and what was the role of trade union organisation in supporting and promoting them? and
- what was the effect of political change on the outcomes of discourse at this level and how did the various interest groups adapt their strategies to deal with the influence of the enormous change in the broader political situation which occurred following the passing of the Act?

If the tripartite system can be shown to have worked as a structure in which representative dialogue on health and safety has led to effective results, then perhaps its extension to include further public and consumer interests may be a way to further advance democratic debate over health and safety regulation. Of course, there are other aspects of representation which need to be addressed before such a view can be confidently advanced. In particular, there are important questions concerning the wider context of such debate and the extent to which economic issues concerning production, profit and markets, not to mention the threat of unemployment and social dumping, underlie decision-making on health and safety issues. There are also many questions about the interests to be included and the support they would need in order to make an informed contribution to decision-making on health and safety issues.

Fundamental to all these questions is the nature of the power relations involved and the extent to which worker and public interest in issues of health and safety can engage with the interests of capital on anything remotely approximating an equal footing. Between the articulation of different perceptions of risk and the acceptance of an eventual decision on its tolerability, lies a complex process in which the strength of interest groups, the allegiances and support they command, and the economic ramifications of possible decisions all figure in influencing outcome. Where trade unions have been successful in this process in the past, it has been at least in part because they have been a single channel for the representation of organised labour which carried with it not only an unchallenged legitimacy but also significant enconomic influence and political strength. This is not the case with regard to the many representatives of social, consumer, small business and professional interests that potentially would have a role in a broadened structure for dialogue on decision-making in health and safety.

At the same time, tripartism is not simply about representing the interests of particular groups. In achieving trade union aims at the level of national decision-making on health and safety, trade union strategies also benefit unorganised workers. Although the decline in trade union recognition and membership over the last two decades weakens their industrial and political strength, arguably, they still remain the only organised and credible voice of workers. While it is desirable to extend consultation structures to include the increasing numbers of unorganised workers engaged in peripheral, temporary or atypical work, as well as wider public, professional and small business interests, it is not clear how this could be best achieved or how their involvement would effect outcomes which would be beneficial to those at risk.

Nevertheless, perhaps there are some lessons that can be learned from the experience of environmental regulation. The success of environmental interest groups in drawing attention to their concerns and influencing wider public opinion suggests that the tripartite model as originally conceived may not be the only way to promote participation in issues concerning occupational and public risk arising from economic activities. Government has gradually come to understand that risk communication involves more than reassurances that experts know best. This has occurred, not because of a unilateral awakening of understanding on the part of the regulators, but precisely because society has demonstrated an increasing lack of confidence in government regulatory decisions based on the old formulae and has placed questions on the freedom of information, accountability and participation on the political agenda. There are many issues that arise from this. One, for example, is the composition of the governing body of the Environment Agency, which is drawn from a wide range of backgrounds and includes representatives from green pressure groups. Whether this kind of approach represents a way forward for participation in decision-making about work-related risks seems to be dependent on a more thorough evaluation of both the experience and potential of the operation of these and similar systems as well as on carrying out the long overdue appraisal of the effectiveness of the system put in place by the HSW Act.

A further area in which more immediate change could be effected is through the regionalisation of the HSC's consultative structures along the lines of the Environmental Protection Advisory Councils (EPACs) set up by the Environment Agency in pursuance of requirements laid down by the Environmental Protection Act. Such regional councils for health and safety could be set up to mirror the HSE regional structure and, as is the case with the EPACs, they could have a statutory right to be consulted and to make representations, thus *inter alia* increasing the local accountbaility of the HSE.

The role of EHOs

EHOs, in terms of the full-time equivalents engaged in health and safety activities, are as numerous as HSE inspectors. They also have enforcement duties in respect of many more workplaces than their HSE counterparts; although these workplaces, for the most part, contain lower risk activities.

The Robens Committee did pay attention to the question of whether the enforcement responsibilities of local authorities, which then related to the requirements of the Offices, Shops and Railway Premises Act 1963, should be included in its proposed new central inspectorate. It, however, concluded that this was neither feasible or desirable. Thus, the Committee argued that local authority enforcement in the health and safety field was a logical extension of its public health role and that combining these two areas of enforcement was economical. It further drew attention to the value of such an enforcement role in stimulating local interest in workplace health and safety[24].

The argument that it is both logical and cost-effective to combine the enforcement of statutory requirements relating to health and safety and public health continues to have some force. At the same time, it also needs to be recognised that the current division of enforcement responsibilities between HSE and local authorities has certain disadvantages. First, it means that across much of the economy health and safety provisions are enforced by inspectors who spend only part of their time dealing with health and safety issues and hence will frequently not possess high levels of specialist competency. Secondly, it is confusing to both employers and unions. Thirdly, it serves to work against the espoused principle of focusing inspector resources on those areas where the risks are highest, notwithstanding the work of HELA in trying to ensure a consistent approach towards enforcement on the part of HSE inspectors and EHOs. For the division precludes any consideration of whether the resource currently deployed on enforcement in local authority areas might not be better focused on those activities for which the HSE has responsibility.

There would consequently seem to be a case for looking again at the desirability (and scale) of the local authority role in the enforcement of health and safety law. In the meantime, given the statistics detailed earlier on the marked variation that exist in enforcement action undertaken in different types of local authorities and other official figures which indicate that similar variations exist in the ratios between EHOs and the number of premises for which they are responsible, two, more immediate, actions appear necessary. These are the taking of further steps to ensure consistency between authorities in the way in which enforcement activities are approached, and the development of national guidance on how EHO staffing levels should be determined.

Any move to remove or reduce the enforcement role of local authorities would clearly be vulnerable to the argument that it represented a reduction in local democracy. This argument could, however, arguably be countered if the above proposal concerning the establishment of HSC regional consultative committees were implemented.

Enforcement strategies and powers

A number of issues appear to merit attention in this area. These are the nature and scale of inspections and investigations, the current approach adopted towards the use of enforcement notices and prosecutions, the present provision made for the prosecution of directors and other senior office holders, the sentencing powers and approach of the courts, and the role to be played by manslaughter prosecutions. Each of these are therefore considered in turn below.

Inspections and investigations. HSE inspectors and EHOs, as has been noted, conduct routine preventive inspections, investigate the causes of injuries and other incidents and also conduct investigations into complaints received. In recent years the last of these sources of work has been increasing and placing growing demands on inspectorate resources. In the case of HSE this has, in turn, created difficulties in terms of resourcing preventive inspections, as well as other types of investigation.

The investigation of complaints is clearly highly important. At the same time the two other types of activity are equally of importance. An adequate programme of preventive inspections, for example, is necessary to ensure that duty holders feel that there is a realistic chance of their health and safety arrangements being checked and also provides inspectors with a valuable source of information on new risks and technological and organisational developments[24]. Similarly, sufficient investigations into the causes of accidents and other incidents need to be conducted to ensure that those who recklessly or negligently harm workers are brought to account.

At present the resources available to the HSE and local authority Environmental Health Departments are not sufficient to enable preventive inspections and the latter type of investigations to be conducted at a level sufficient to fulfil these objectives. In the case of inspections, one solution utilised to deal with the problem has been to focus greater attention on "higher risk" workplaces. In recent years this approach has been further accentuated by a tendency to devote more resources to the carrying out of more in-depth inspections in larger such workplaces.

In the context of limited resources, focusing inspections on the more hazardous workplaces makes sense. Such an approach, however, is not a substitute for an adequate programme of preventive inspections. Indeed, the presence of such a programme is a necessary pre-condition for the development of an informed approach to targeting. This is for two, related, reasons. First, it provides the "intelligence" needed to identify "high risk" workplaces. Secondly, it provides a means of ensuring that the data so gathered is regularly updated and in this way ensures that any change in the "riskiness" of the activities undertaken in a particular premises is recorded and fed back into the targeting process.

In short, "targeting" ameliorates the consequences of inadequate staffing levels. It does not, however, provide an effective long-term solution to them. Given this, there seems no alternative other than to significantly increase the number of inspectors available to carry out inspections, as well as investigations (see below). At the same time, insofar as resources remain highly constrained, there seems a case for looking again at the advantages and disadvantages associated with conducting fewer more in-depth inspections, as opposed to carrying out a greater number of less sophisticated ones. In addition, consideration could be given to supplementing the activities of HSE inspectors and EHOs through the imposition of statutory requirements aimes at stimulating greater "independent" monitoring of employer health and safety arrangements.

Recently Gunningham and Johnstone have raised the possibility of introducing a two-track approach to the regulation of health and safety management[25]. Under "Track Two" employers who introduced Safety Management Systems (SMSs) would be rewarded through the provision of various "incentives", such as a reduced likelihood of inspections and prosecutions, less prescriptive regulatory requirements and lower penalties, if prosecutions take place. In contrast, the activities of "Track One" employers, that is those who have not adopted SMSs, would continue to be regulated in the traditional way.

This approach could potentially enable inspectors to devote more time to those employers who manage health and safety in a less sophisticated and comprehensive way. However, the risks of what Gunningham and Johnstone refer to as "implementation failure" seem to us too great, particularly given that many likely "Track Two" employers would be engaged in high risk areas of activity, to consider reducing the degree to which they are externally regulated. Nevertheless, one aspect of their proposal does seem worth exploring. This is the imposition of requirements on employers, or at least those who are above a specified size and/or who are engaged in particularly high risk types of activity, to have their health and safety arrangements regularly audited by accredited outside bodies – bodies that could include the sectoral insurance associations proposed in chapter 5, and which would be under a duty to carry out their work with "due diligence". The results of these audits, could then be made available to the HSE (as well as worker representatives) and be used to guide future inspection and enforcement action.

Finally, with regard to the investigation of accidents and other incidents, it is a truism to say that inspectors need to know that they have occurred in order for them to initiate an investigation. At present HSE inspectors and EHOs rely on employers to report injuries, dangerous occurrences and occupational diseases in accordance with the Reporting of Injuries, Diseases and Dangerous Occurrences Regulations. Unfortunately, as already noted, the majority of incidents that should be reported are not. This may in part be due to the fact that employers are unaware of their reporting obligations. It may also be partly due to their concluding that it is not in their interests to make a required report. In any event it is clear that the self-reporting system is not working adequately. As a result there seems a need for HSC/HSE to further develop systems to encourage people, other that employers, to report injuries to them – like doctors, hospitals, solicitors, trade unions, insurance companies and the police.

Notices and prosecutions. As we have seen, it is relatively uncommon for an enforcement notice to be issued following an inspection and even rarer for a prosecution to be instigated. This is despite the fact that the available evidence indicates that many employers remain unaware of their legal obligations and hence are not likely to be complying with them (see chapter 2).

Neither the HSC or the HSE are concerned about this situation. The HSC, for example, takes the view that its priority is prevention and that this objective is best served by an inspector at first working with duty holders to gain compliance with the law. Only when advice has not been taken should an inspector consider the imposition of notices or prosecution.

This philosophy of compliance reflects the approach taken by the Robens Committee which concluded that "only flagrant breaches of the law" should be prosecuted. In doing so it observed that:

"...the process of prosecution and punishment by the criminal courts is largely an irrelevancy. The real need is for a constructive means of ensuring that practical improvements are made and preventive measures adopted. Whatever the value of the threat of prosecution, that actual process of prosecution makes little direct contribution towards the end. On the contrary, the laborious work of preparing prosecutions... consumes much valuable time which inspectorates are naturally reluctant to devote to such little purpose"[26].

"Technical problems of safety organisation and accident prevention are matters for experts in the industrial field rather than the courts... the weight of the evidence points to the conclusion that the lengthy process of investigation, warning, institution of criminal proceedings, conviction and ultimate fine is not a very effective way of producing an early remedy for known unsatisfactory conditions. In sum we do not believe that the traditional sanction demands any widespread degree of respect or confidence in this field"[27].

The HSC's current enforcement policy, as shall be seen, differs some-what from the approach advocated by the Robens Committee. Nevertheless, HSE enforcement activities, as the above evidence indi-cates, does incorporate relatively limited use of prosecutions as well as enforcement notices. This approach is problematic for a variety of reasons. First, it constitutes more an article of faith than an approach to enforcement that has been empirically demonstrated to be the most effective. The HSE, for example, has not conducted any research into whether advice or more formal legal action is the most effective method to ensure improvements take place – although it is currently conducting several studies concerned with assessing "the best possi-ble balance between the various regulatory measures" that are cur-rently used. Secondly, and relatedly, it is far from clear that enforce-ment notices are any less cost-effective than the provision of informal advisory letters. Thirdly, it seems strange that a State agency should in effect adopt an enforcement strategy premised on effectively pro-viding a free consultancy service to those who choose not to find out about the law and fail to take the action needed to comply with it. Fourthly, as shown in chapter 2, the present enforcement strategy does not seem to have encouraged a willingness on the part of many employers to take their health and safety responsibilities seriously. Finally, the appropriateness of such a philosophy to an environment where inspector numbers are simply not adequate to ensure that advice is provided regularly to a large proportion of employers must be questionable. For such advice is essentially a private matter between an inspector and employer and hence, unlike a prosecution, or even an enforcement notice, is unlikely to draw the attention of other org-anisations to the need to accord health and safety a higher priority.

In fact this last point receives support in a set of considerations which the HSC issued in 1998 to provide guidance to inspectors as to when a prosecution should be initiated[28]. Thus, these state that:

"The Commission expects that enforcing authorities will consider prosecution when

- it is appropriate in the circumstances as a way to draw attention to the need for compliance with the law and the maintenance of standards required by the law, where there would be a normal expectation that a prosecution would be taken or whether, through the conviction of offenders, others may be deterred from similar failures to comply with the law;
- or there is judged to have been potential for considerable harm arising from a breach;

- or the gravity of the offence, taken together with the general record and approach of the offender warrants it, for example apparent reckless disregard for standards, repeated breaches, persistent poor standards."

Strikingly, the first heading could mean that almost every breach of the law discovered by an inspector could merit prosecution. For it could be argued in relation to almost every breach either that (a) "it is appropriate in the circumstances as a way to draw attention to the need for compliance with the law", or (b) that "there would be a normal expectation that a prosecution would be taken", or (c) that "through the conviction of offenders, others may be deterred from similar failures to comply with the law."

This is not to argue that all breaches of the law should be prosecuted. Indeed it is recognised that inspectors need to possess some discretion as to whether or not prosecution constitutes the most appropriate action in a given situation. Rather it is to suggest that a much more rigorous approach to enforcement needs to be adopted. Clearly there is scope for debate about the nature of such a revised approach[29]. However, in our view it should encompass:

- the issuing of an enforcement notice in all cases where a serious risk of personal injury exists;
- more frequent use of prosecutions combined with a greater willingness to take cases on indictment; and
- a policy of prosecuting wherever a breach of the law is found to have resulted in a major injury or death on the grounds that unlawful conduct which results in harm requires retribution in a way that other such conduct does not.

It is recognised that the taking of more prosecutions, particularly on indictment, would entail the use of more HSE and EHO resources – an issue to which we return below. It is also acknowledged that some trade-off will always exist in terms of the allocation of inspection time between prosecutions, on the one hand, and inspections and investigations, on the other. However, the scale of this trade-off could be reduced, although probably to a limited degree, by the government allowing any fines imposed, and costs awarded, to be given to local authorities and the HSE. Its potentially adverse consequences could also be ameliorated by providing workers and unions with the right to bring private prosecutions without needing to obtain the consent of the Director of Public Prosecutions.

Prosecution of directors. As noted earlier, at present few prosecutions are currently brought against directors and other senior officers of corporate bodies. The importance of bringing directors to account through the criminal court is too often overlooked. Apart from it being important that directors should not be seen to be above the law and escape criminal accountability, the backbone of any system of deterrence, in relation to preventing corporate harm, must be action against those in control of the company. As Braithwaite and Geis have stated,

"White collar criminals are among the most deterrable types of offenders because they satisfy two conditions. They do not have a commitment to crime as a way of life, and their offences are instrumental rather than expressive. Corporate crimes are almost never crimes of passion; they are not spontaneous or emotional, but calculated risks taken by rational actors. As such they should be more amenable to control by policies based on the utilitarian assumption of the deterrence doctrine.... Individual corporate criminals are also more deterrable because they have more of those valued possessions that can be lost through a criminal conviction, such as social status, respectability, money, a job and a comfortable home and family life.[30]"

The low level of prosecutions is admittedly not simply the HSE's failure. It also reflects weaknesses in the present law.

The provisions of section 37 of the HSW Act enabling such prosecutions are virtually useless as a means of bringing proceedings against the senior officials of large corporations because of the difficulty of showing the necessary fault on their part. Furthermore, this evidential problem is compounded by case law relating to the meaning of "neglect" which indicates that there is no obligation on directors to ensure positively that their company is abiding by health and safety law or indeed to ensure that those to whom they have delegated safety duties are carrying them out. Thus, in the 1970 case of *Huckerby v Elliott*, Lord Parker observed:

"I know of no authority for the proposition that it is the duty of a director to, as it were, supervise his co-directors or to acquaint himself with all of the details of the running of a company. Indeed it has been said [in another case] that amongst other things it is perfectly proper for a director to leave matters to another director or to an official of the company and that he is under no obligation to test the accuracy of anything that he is told by such a person or even to make sure that he is complying with the law"[31].

This situation contrasts sharply with the stringent fiduciary duties that a director owes his company under company law: the negligent breach of which can lead to a period of imprisonment of up to seven years. The obvious solution to the weaknesses of section 37 is therefore to follow this approach and impose an explicit duty on directors in relation to health and safety. Such a duty could be formulated along the following lines: "It is the duty of the nominated director to define, implement and monitor health and safety so as to ensure to the standards set down by the law, that the company's activities are managed and organised to ensure the health and safety of person's who may be affected by their activities"[32].

The imposition of this duty could be supported by a further legal change. This is to remove the current restrictions on the use of imprisonment as a penalty for breaches of health and safety law. That is to make imprisonment a possible sentence for all individual convictions. Such a change, it should be noted, is apparently currently under consideration by the government[33].

Sentencing. Almost all parties with an interest in health and safety are in an agreement on one point: courts impose far too lenient sentences. The recent decision in *R v Howe* may, as noted earlier, be having a beneficial impact in terms of addressing this situation[34]. It nevertheless needs to be recognised that the Howe decision does have its limitation.

Though the court did state that any "fine should reflect not only the gravity of the offence but also the means of the offender", it specifically ruled out that the fine "should bear any specific relationship to the [company's] turnover or net profit." It further did not suggest that the courts should, on a routine basis, receive information about the financial affairs of the company, but merely observed that a company may choose to supply this information to the court when it "wished to make any submission... about its ability to pay a fine."

It is consequently perhaps time that consideration be given to "proportionate" or "percentage" fines for companies[35]. This concept is well known under European Community law – now enshrined in British law. Thus, under the competition law provisions, a (civil) fine of up to 10% of the company's previous global turnover can be imposed.

Proportionate fining could work in the following way. Different crimes would each have a separate percentage level attached to it – increasing with the seriousness of the offence. The court would then multiply the percentage level of the offence for which the company has been convicted with a figure representing the profits of the company averaged out over the last five years. Courts could then be given discretion to depart from this formulae in certain specified types of circumstance.

Sentencing companies to large "cash" fines does have one potential drawback – the problem of "overspill". This means that companies can pass the fine on to workers, through redundancy or wage cuts, or to customers through increasing the price of goods or services. Equity fines are one ingenious solution to this "overspill phenomenon" for publicly listed companies.

The US academic John Coffee suggests that when "very severe fines need to be imposed on a corporation, they should be imposed not in cash, but in the equity securities of the corporation". The convicted would be required to issue a particular number of shares – equivalent to an expected market value to the cash fine necessary. Coffee then suggests that these shares would be placed in the state's crime victim's compensation fund to be used when required. This would allow much higher fines to be imposed since, the court,

> "seizes not just whatever cash the company has available to pay a fine or monetary penalty but also a share in future earnings, as well as ownership rights in the company's plant, equipment and property investments.[36]"

Monetary sentences – whether expressed as cash or equity fines – nevertheless do have limitations; they do not deal with the "rehabilitation" of the company. Unlike the minds of individuals which can't be re-modelled, the components of a company can be analysed and reformed. New polices can be adopted, new job positions created and new systems of organisation set up. The organisational defects of a company – its 'psyche' – can be taken to pieces and put together. Unsafe companies can be turned into safe ones.

Since the enactment of the 1984 Sentencing Reform Act in the United States, companies are frequently sentenced to "corporate probation". The Act allows probation orders to be used as a substitute, or an addition, to fines. Conditions of probation no longer need be limited to rehabilitative ends and can be imposed for purposes of increasing punishment or deterrence.

Before a court can issue a probation order, a pre-sentence report must be prepared. This report can address sources of illegal behaviour by a corporate defendant and recommend terms of a probation sentence. Should a sentencing court want more information it may order a study of the offender by qualified professional consultants; these reports need not be limited to factual inquiries, but can also include analyses of possible probation sentences. Consultants qualified to perform such studies include business professionals or academics with expertise concerning management techniques. Pre-sentencing reports and studies can therefore provide a court with key information about the internal management processes that led to the defendant's illegal conduct and hence the changes that would help prevent a recurrence.

In Britain, such a power might be considered unnecessary since the HSE has the power to impose changes on the companies after the incident leading to the conviction. However, inspectors often only have the power to require superficial changes to a company's operations. Yet company procedures may need deep-rooted reforms to ensure that the offence does not happen again. Corporate probation provides a potential means of securing such reforms. For example, new training schemes could be required, management structures revised, and new safety officers employed or new standing orders drafted.

The HSW Act does, as already noted, give courts the power to issue a "remedy order" which could provide the basis for a more sophisticated probation order. In addition, the Law Commission has proposed that courts have the power to issue a remedial order for companies convicted of its proposed offence of corporate killing. This proposal, though a move in the right direction, is very limited. First, it is only relevant when a company is convicted of the Law Commission's proposed offence. Secondly, it is framed too narrowly. The court can only "order the corporation to take such steps... for remedying the failure in question and any matter which appears to the court to have resulted from the failure and been the cause or one of the causes of the death." Finally, the court can only give an order if the prosecution itself makes an application specifying the terms of the requested order. Although the court should be able to act on the basis of a prosecution application, it should also have the power to make its own order without any application.

The manslaughter protocol. It is unclear how effective the new manslaughter protocol will be. Formal police involvement is clearly an important step forward. However, it is not clear how much difference it will actually make. The police need to carry out a parallel enquiry to the HSE, not just make an "initial assessment" as the protocol requires. How can a police officer make a proper assessment of whether a company director has committed manslaughter without actually conducting an investigation? As Detective Chief Superintendent Bill Hacking, an ACPO representative says, "[i]t is only after a major investigation by the police, and possibly other agencies, that an apparent act of negligence or recklessness is identified. Past experience has also shown that in the early stages of an investigation the full facts are not always revealed". If this is the case, why then does the protocol not require more than this "initial assessment"? In addition, CID officers are not provided with proper training in the investigation of this form of corporate crime.

Since it is highly unlikely that without a formal police investigation, a police detective will find the "circumstances that might justify a charge of manslaughter", the system is likely to rely on HSE inspectors deciding, during the course of their investigations, whether to refer a case back to the police. It is highly questionable, however, whether HSE inspectors properly filter out all potential corporate manslaughter cases. HSE inspectors are under huge work pressure with the result that, although they spend time investigating a workplace death, they are constantly aware that their investigation is at the expense of other preventative inspection work. Unless director culpability is staring them in the face, inspectors neither have the time, or the forensic experience, to uncover the complicity of senior managers and directors, particularly if the death took place in a large company. As a result there is a great likelihood that many appropriate cases will not be referred.

Manslaughter law. As the law stands, a company can only be convicted for the offence of manslaughter (or indeed for any other conventional crime of violence) if a person considered to be a "guiding mind and will" of the company, is convicted for the offence. The guilt or innocence of the *company* therefore rests upon guilt or innocence of this individual – who must be a director or senior manager. If this person is guilty as an individual for the offence in question, the company is automatically convicted (assuming it has been charged).

This doctrine – known as the "identification" doctrine – has been the subject of great criticism. It allows companies whose policies and procedures are "reckless" or "grossly negligent" to remain unconvicted simply because there is insufficient evidence against a senior officer. Even if there was a director who could be prosecuted for this offence, a combination of inadequate investigation by the authorities and the absence of clear cut duties can often make it difficult to pinpoint criminal responsibility upon directors or other senior officers. In addition, as Clarkson states:

> "In larger companies with complex structures, decision making is usually the product of corporate policy and procedures and in as much as decisions are ever made by one person (which is necessary under the identification doctrine), it will usually be a manager of a section who will not be regarded as senior enough for the purposes of the identification doctrine."[37]

The doctrine therefore allows companies – with grossly negligent management operations – to escape conviction simply because there is insufficient evidence to convict a director or senior company officer.

In 1996, the Law Commission proposed the enactment of a new offence of "corporate killing – which would replace the existing offence of corporate manslaughter. Under this a company would be convicted if it can be shown that "a management failure by the corporation is the cause or one of the causes of a person's death" and "that failure constitutes conduct falling far below what can reasonably be expected of the Corporation in the circumstances"

The Law Commission's concept of "management failure" at the heart of the new offence is a clever way of removing the need to consider individual guilt, and does get to grip with the 'corporateness" of company culpability. It is therefore to be welcomed that the HSC has indicated its support for the new offence and that the government is currently looking at the Law Commission's proposal in detail.

The Commission did not, however, propose to amend the identification doctrine as the general principle of determining corporate liability – despite identifying a number of significant problems with the principle. The government should therefore also consider whether the new "management failure" test should be applied to all conventional crimes of violence committed by a company[38].

HSE resources

DURING the first 13 years of the Conservative Government, the HSE's budget was significantly reduced in real terms. Moreover from 1993 onwards, it was effectively frozen, resulting in much lower rates of recruitment and the early retirement of a number of the most experienced inspectors. With the Labour government's return to power, this position is now being reversed; the government is providing the HSE with an additional £63 million over three years. However, much of this new money is generated by the imposition of charges (under the COMAH regulations, amongst others) for such things as safety cases and regulatory visits[39]. There is as yet nothing to suggest that the HSE is going to be successful in collecting those charges. If the HSE does not manage to collect them it will be doubly penalised in that it will have to expend money in legal action to effect recovery and the government will not provide additional finance to cover uncollected charges.

Although the HSE intends to increase the number of inspectors by over a hundred by April 2000, this increase will not make much of a dent in the number of uninspected workplaces or in the number of injuries that are not investigated. A larger increase in inspector numbers consequently appears necessary, not least because HSE figures for 1995/96 suggest that if the planned increase was focused solely in FOD, it would only result in the carrying out of around 36,000 additional inspections. Such an increase would moreover almost certainly mean that FOD (in combination with the current

Chemical and Hazardous Installations Directorate) would still be carrying out fewer inspections than in 1991/92[40].

The need for a considerable expansion of HSE inspection resources is further supported by the following:

- the employment of less than 15 inspectors to cover the mining industry, an industry which, although much smaller than previously, now contains, as a result of privatisation, a multiplicity of employers and consequently a much greater variation in health and safety standards;

- the presence of around 15 inspectors to enforce the law in the expanding and highly hazardous quarrying industry;

- a railway inspectorate that has just 22 inspectors working in the field to supervise a large number of train operating companies whose activities interface to a large extent – Crewe station, for example, is used by somewhere in the region of 24 different companies; and

- as already noted, the employment within EMAS of just 50-60 doctors and nurses to cover a workforce of 27 million – a staffing level which both precludes them from taking on a role similar to HSE "specialist inspectors" and severely limits the role they can play in encouraging and assisting employers to set up their own occupational health services to deal with the very considerable health problems caused by business activities (see chapter 5).

The HSE's need for increased funding, however, extends beyond the employment of additional inspectors. Thus, additional resources are also needed to support the proposed move to a more rigorous approach to enforcement and to expand the amount of research that the HSE undertakes and commissions.

Such a large increase in HSE resources will clearly not be easily achieved. It, however, needs to be placed in the context of the fact that its annual cost to the taxpayer totals around £190 million, a figure that represents less than 0.01% of government expenditure. It also needs to be considered in relation to estimates which suggest that work-related injuries and ill health cost society as a whole between £11 billion and £16 billion a year[41].

Conclusion

THE way in which a statutory framework of law is administered exerts a crucial influence over both its operation and effectiveness. In Britain, three main groups of actors are involved in this administrative process – the HSC, the HSE and EHOs employed by local authorities. This chapter has consequently examined the roles, resources and activities of these actors.

The chapter acknowledges the important contribution of the HSW Act in terms of creating the HSC, as a central authority for health and safety of work, and establishing the HSE as its operational arm. At the same time, however, it draws attention to a variety of problems that exist in relation to the administration of the legal framework established by the Act. These include, inadequate levels of preventive inspections and investigations; the placing of too greater reliance on the provision of advice and the use of other informal methods of securing legal compliance; the imposition of overly low penalties following successful prosecutions; insufficient levels of research funding; and a lack of occupational health expertise within the HSE.

A range of proposals have therefore been put forward to remedy these problems. These are summarised below and relate to five main issues: the structure of the HSC; the responsibilities of the HSE in respect of public health and safety; the role of local authorities in enforcing health and safety law; the adequacy of current enforcement strategies and powers; and HSE resources.

Summary of key points

Administration of the statutory framework

- investigation into the effectiveness of the tripartite structure of the Health and Safety Commission (HSC) in order to evaluate whether there is a case for expanding its membership to encompass a wider range of interest groups;
- establishment of a system of HSC regional consultative committees along the lines of the Environmental Protection Advisory Councils set up by the Environment Agency;
- investigation into desirability (and scale) of local authority involvement in the enforcement of health and safety law
- action to achieve greater consistency between local authorities in terms of enforcement action and Environmental Health Officer staffing levels;
- adoption of a more rigorous enforcement policy on the part of HSE and local authority inspectors, and within this the placing of more emphasis on the use of prosecutions combined with a greater willingness to take cases on indictment;
- supplementation of HSE and local authority inspections by the introduction of statutory requirements on the carrying out of "third party" audits on employer health and safety arrangements and performance;
- imposition of an explicit health and safety duty on company directors;
- removal of current restrictions on the use of imprisonment as a penalty for breaches of health and safety law;
- possible introduction of "proportionate" and "equity" fines for health and safety offences and the use of pre-sentencing reports;
- provision of court powers to make probation orders requiring organisations to take specified steps to improve their health and safety arrangements;
- strengthening of the current protocol on the investigation of workplace deaths along with the introduction of the Law Commission's proposed offence of "corporate killing";
- enhanced right for workers and their trade unions to initiate private prosecutions in respect of breaches of health and safety laws;
- considerable expansion of HSE resources to support a substantial increase in inspectors, support the adoption of a more rigorous enforcement policy and an expansion in internal and commissioned research.

Notes

1 See eg. T. Nichols, *"The Sociology of Industrial Injury"*, 1997, Mansell; and R. Moore, *"The Price of Safety: the market, workers' rights and the law"*, 1992, Institute of Employment Rights.

2 See eg. P. Bartrip and S. Burman, *"The Wounded Soldiers of Industry: Industrial Compensation Policy 1830-1897"*, 1983, Clarendon.

3 Health and Safety (Enforcing Authority) Regulations 1998 (SI 1998 No.494)

4 See eg. P. James, "Occupational health and Safety: The Impact of European Requirements", *Review of Employment Topics*, 3(1), 1995, 74-102.

5 Unless otherwise stated, the figures provided on inspector staffing and activities are taken from the following sources: Health and Safety Commission Annual Reports and Accounts 1997/98, 1998, HSE Books; and Health and Safety Commission, National Picture of Health and Safety in the Local Authority Enforced Sectors, 1999, Health and Safety Executive.

6 P. James, "The enforcement record of the HSE's Field Operations Division", *Health and Safety Bulletin*, 261, 1997, 9-12.

7 Reporting of Injuries, Diseases and Dangerous Occurrences Regulations 1995 (SI 1995 No. 3163).

8 Health and Safety Commission, 1999, op cit, p.40.

9 Calculated from HSE statistics (HSE Statistics Office).

10 The HSE does not provide this information in a way that allows for an exact number

11 B. Hutter and S. Lloyd-Bostock, "The Power of Accidents: The Social and Psychological Impact of Accidents and the Enforcement of Safety Regulations", *British Journal of Criminology*, 30, 1990, 409-422.

12 *R v F Howe & Son (Engineers)* [1997] 28 IRLR 434-438.

13 D. Bergman, (1994), *"The Perfect Crime? How Companies can Get away with Manslaughter in the Workplace"* published by the West Midlands Health and Safety Advice Centre (tel: 0121 236 0801).

14 See eg. "Company director faces jail sentence for tampering with fatal accident evidence", *Health and Safety Bulletin*, 250, June 1997, 2

15 For discussion of all the HSE arguments see David Bergman, *The Perfect Crime* (West Midlands Health and Safety Advice Centre) op cit

16 *"Overlapping Enforcement Responsibility: Relations between the HSE and DPP, the Crown Prosecution Service and the Police"*.

17 *"Guidance to Inspectors on Possible Manslaughter Cases."* Para 7, HSE Document OC 165/5

18 The figure 56 includes referrals of deaths to members of the public which are not included in the total of 1,441 deaths. There were three referrals in 1992/3; two in 1993/4; three in 1994/5; four in 1995/6; six in 1996/7 and five 1997/8. (HSE, statistics: see D. Bergman, "Directors Duties Deterrence", *Health and Safety Bulletin*, Dec. 1998.

19 G. Slapper, (1999), *Blood in the Bank*, (Assignee)

20 See *Health and Safety Executive, Mainstream Research Market 1999/2000*, 1999, HSE

21 A.J.P. Dalton, (1992) Lessons from the United Kingdom: Fightback on workplace hazards, *International Journal of Health Services*, vol 22, no 3, pp.489-495

22 Department of the Environment, Transport and the Regions/Health and

---

Safety Commission (1999), Revitalising Health and Safety Consultation Document, DETR. J. Rimington, (1999) HSW Act 25-year service, *Occupational Health Review*, 81, pp.12-15, IRS

23 J. Locke, (1981) *The Politics of Health and Safety*, Sir Alexander Redgrave Memorial Lecture, IOSH; also summarised in *Protection*, July 1981

24 B. Hutter, "An Inspector Calls: The Importance of Proactive Enforcement in the Regulatory Context", *British Journal of Criminology*, 26(2), 1986, 114-129.

25 N. Gunningham, and R. Johnstone, *Regulating Workplace Safety: Systems and Sanctions*, 1999, Oxford University Press

26 Lord Robens, 1972, para 261.

27 Ibid.

28 See *Enforcement Handbook, HSE*, 1 April 1998, chapter 1.

29 See F. Pearce and S. Tombs, "Policing Corporate 'Skid Rows'", *British Journal of Criminology*, 31(4), 1991, 415-426; and K. Hawkins, "Enforcing Regulation: More of the Same from Pearce and Tombs", *British Journal of Criminology*, 31(4), 1991, 427-430.

30 J. Braithwaite and G. Geis, "Theory and Action for Corporate Crime Control", *Crime and Delinquency*, April 82, 292, at p302

31 *Hukerby v Elliott* [1970] All ER at p.194.

32 See D. Bergman, "Directors, duties and deterrence", *Health and Safety Bulletin*, December 1998, p.11

33 See *"Revitalising Health and Safety"*, HSC/DETR Consultation Document, July 1999, p.21. imprisonment.

34 See HSE press Release, 30 July 1999 "Record of three big health and safety fines this week"

35 See J. Coffee, "No Soul to Damn: No body to Kick" An unscandalised inquiry into the Problem of Corporate Punishment" 79 *Michigan Law Review* (1981), 386, at 413. See also D. Bergman, "Crime and punishment", *Health & Safety Bulletin*, 275, Jan/Feb 1999, pp13-16

36 B. Fisse 1 *Criminal Law Forum* 211 at 231

37 Clarkson (1998) 2 *Web Journal of Current Legal Issues*

38 See Disaster Action (1999) *"Corporate Violence and the Criminal Justice System"*, (forthcoming)

39 See "HSE to receive £63m three-year boost", *Health and Safety Bulletin*, 276, March 1999, 2.

40 James, 1997, op cit.

41 N. Davies and P. Teasdale, *"The Costs to the British Economy of Work Accidents and Work-Related Diseases"*, 1994, HSE Books.

Chapter 4

Worker representation

THE collective involvement of workers in the monitoring and development of health and safety arrangements at the workplace has long been viewed as a valuable means of improving standards of worker protection[1]. The available research evidence moreover indicates that this view is well-founded. Thus, a variety of studies, conducted both in this country and overseas, have found the collective representation of workers to have beneficial consequences for standards of worker protection, particularly when it is trade union based[2]. In addition, several of these have highlighted the fact that injury rates tend to be highest in workplaces where there is unilateral determination of health and safety by management[3].

Statutory provisions designed to support and encourage such representation were first introduced in Britain in the coal mining industry at the end of the nineteenth century. However, a general legal framework relating to it was only established following the advent of the HSW Act. Subsequently, this framework, as is shown below, has been amended in a number of important respects, most notably through its extension to non-unionised workplaces and workers.

Any study of whether current health and safety laws should be reformed must, given the above research findings, pay attention to the adequacy of these provisions on worker representation and possible means of improving them. The present chapter provides such an evaluation.

Initially the present legal framework for worker representation is briefly outlined. The operation of this framework is then reviewed and various ways in which it could be improved considered. Finally, a number of proposals for reform are put forward.

The present legal framework

THE Robens committee laid great emphasis on the importance of workforce involvement in health and safety matters and indeed saw such involvement as a central component in the development of greater self-regulation within industry. It recommended that its use should be encouraged by placing a statutory duty on all employers to consult with "employees or their representatives at the workplace on measures for promoting safety and health at work, and to provide arrangements for the participation of employees in the development of such measures"[4].

In the event, a rather different approach to the issue of workforce involvement was adopted in the HSW Act. Instead of imposing a general duty of consultation on employers, the Act, via sections 2(4), 2(5) and 2(7), provided for regulations to be made under which (a) recognised trade unions could appoint safety representatives (b) the workforce could elect such representatives and (c) these representatives could request the establishment of health and safety committees. In addition, where safety representatives were so appointed or elected, it further, by virtue of section 2(6), obliged an employer to consult them "with a view to the making and maintenance of arrangements which will enable him and his employees to co-operate effectively in promoting and developing measures to ensure the health and safety at work of the employees, and in checking the effectiveness of such measures".

Subsequently, as a result of pressure from the trade union movement, section 2(5) was repealed and along with it the power to make regulations for the workforce election of safety representatives. Provisions relating to the appointment and role of safety representatives appointed by recognised trade unions were, however, introduced in the form of the Safety Representatives and Safety Committees (SRSC) Regulations 1977. These regulations, which are supported by two ACOPs, remain in force[5]. However, as shall be seen, they have been amended in several ways.

The SRSC Regulations

The SRSC Regulations enable a union to appoint safety representatives from among the employees of an employer by whom it recognised: although the need for representatives to be appointed from amongst employees does not apply in the case of the British Actors' Equity Association and the Musicians Union. Once appointed in accordance with the regulations representatives acquire a number of "functions". These encompass representing employees in consultation with employers under section 2(6) of the HSW Act; investigating potential hazards and dangerous occurrences; examining the causes of accidents; investigating complaints; making representations to the employer; carrying out workplace inspections; representing employees in consultations with inspectors; receiving information from inspectors in accordance with section 28(8) of the HSW Act; and attending safety committee meetings.

Workplace inspections may be conducted at least every three months. In addition, a further right to inspect arises if there has been a substantial change in the conditions of work or and new information has been published by the HSE relevant to the hazards of the workplace. Inspections can also be conducted to determine the cause of notifiable accidents, dangerous occurrences or diseases and representatives are additionally entitled to inspect and take copies of statutory health and safety documents.

Employers are required, subject to certain qualifications, to make available to representatives information which is necessary to enable them to fulfill their functions. They are also obliged to provide representatives with paid time off to perform their functions and to undergo such training as may be reasonable in the circumstances, having regard to the provisions of a supporting ACOP on the subject. Finally, employers must establish a safety committee if requested to do so by two or more representatives.

Non-SRSC rights of representation

There have been two significant developments since the advent of the SRSC Regulations which have attempted to extend the rights of employees to consultation and representation on health and safety. However, since both were adopted under Conservative governments, whose wider political agenda on employment relations was overtly hostile to trade union representation, it is not surprising that these developments contained little to encourage trade unions.

In 1990, as a result of the Piper Alpha disaster(26), the Offshore Installations (Safety Representatives and Safety Committees) Regulations 1989 were introduced, after many years of disagreement between government, trade unions and the offshore oil industry about the application of British health and safety provisions offshore. These regulations make provision for safety representatives to be elected from all workers in a constituency system and accord those so elected with a variety of rights which, in broad terms, equate with those laid down under the 1977.

A further development, the introduction of the Health and Safety (Consultation with Employees) Regulations 1996 occurred as a result of the need to bring domestic law into line with the requirements of the EU Framework Directive relating to workforce consultation and participation. The recognition of this need was, however, rather belated.

Initially the view was taken, by the HSC, as well as the CBI and the TUC, that the Framework Directive's requirements merely required amendments to be made to the SRSC Regulations and the provision of certain employment protection rights. Representatives and safety committee members, who had been either appointed in pursuance of statutory requirements or recognised by an employer as fulfilling such roles, were therefore, under the Employment Rights Act 1996, given a right of complaint to an employment tribunal if they were dismissed or subjected to a detriment in certain circumstances[6]. In addition, the Schedule to the MHSW regulations made two changes to the 1977 regulatory regime. First, a duty was imposed on employers to provide 'such facilities and assistance as safety representatives may reasonably require for the purpose of carrying out their functions'. Secondly, it was made clear that the duty of consultation laid down under section 2(6) of the HSW Act extended to consulting representatives in 'good time' over the following matters: the introduction of measures which may substantially affect the health and safety of employees; the arrangements for appointing or nominating competent purses in accordance with the MHSW regulations; any health and safety information that had by law to be provided; the planning and organisation of any, similarly required, health and safety training; and the health and safety consequences of new technologies.

Two European Court decisions concerning the UK's failure to fully implement the EC's acquired rights and collective redundancy directives subsequently highlighted the fact that the above changes were insufficient[7]. For they left in place a situation under which employers were only required to consult in situations where unions were recognised. As a result the 1996 HSCE Regulations were introduced to deal with this problem.

The HSCE Regulations require employers to consult with employees not covered by representatives appointed in accordance with the SRSC Regulations. This duty of consultation encompasses the same matters as those specified in the latter regulations. However, employers are given discretion as to whether they consult employees directly or via elected representatives, know as Representatives of Employee Safety (RES).

If the representative route is chosen, employers are required to provide representatives with such information as is necessary to (a) enable them to fully and effectively participate in consultations, and (b) carry out their functions of making representations and consulting with inspectors. They are further required to provide them with such training as is reasonable in the circumstances; such other facilities and assistance as they may reasonably require to carry out their functions; and paid time off to perform these functions and undergo training. The functions of representatives, however, do not include the carrying out of workplace inspections, the inspection of statutory health and safety documents and the investigation of notifiable accidents, diseases and dangerous occurrences. Nor do they provide representatives with a right to request the establishment of a safety committee.

In addition, in contrast to the offshore regulations, the regulations say little on how employers should make arrangements for the election of worker representatives. In particular, they are silent on such matters as the frequency with which elections should be held, the defining of electoral constituencies and the way in which elections should be conducted. These weaknesses are, in turn, compounded by the fact that the regulations are supported by official guidance rather than an ACOP.

In short, the HSCE Regulations represent a minimalist and essentially cosmetic approach to bringing domestic law into line with the requirements of the Framework Directive. As a result, as shall be discussed in more detail below, they cannot be seen to provide a regulatory base for the establishment of effective workplace representation over health and safety matters[8].

Operation of the statutory framework

A good deal of research evidence exists concerning the operation and implementation of the SRSC Regulations. In contrast, only one in-depth study has been carried out on the operation of the offshore regulations relating to safety representatives and committees, and that was conducted fairly shortly after they came into force[9], and no detailed information is available on the HSCE Regulations. As a result attention here is focussed primarily on the operation of the SRSC Regulations. However, some discussion is also provided on the likely effectiveness of the 1996 regulations.

Coverage of safety representatives

In 1979 the HSE undertook a survey which indicated that approximately 79% of employees had access to safety representatives and 75% of them worked in enterprises where joint health and safety committees were present[10]. Against a background of declining levels of trade union recognition and membership, however, a subsequent HSE commissioned survey carried out in 1987 suggested that the coverage of representatives over the intervening period had at best remained static. Thus, it found that the above figures had fallen to 75% and 70% respectively and further revealed that the coverage of safety representatives had declined in smaller workplaces and sectors such as construction and agriculture[11].

Neither of these surveys covered a representative sample of employment and consequently their results need to be treated with caution. In addition, their findings provide a rather less impressive picture if attention is paid to the proportion of workplaces where safety representatives had been appointed. For example, the 1987 survey found that such representatives were present in just 9% of the 4,761 workplaces surveyed.

More recently, the TUC has estimated that 60% of workers had potential access to a safety representative in 1995[12]. This was, however, an indirect estimate based on the proportion of workers in workplaces where trade unions were recognised by employers. It is therefore likely to have been overly optimistic given the likelihood that representatives had not been appointed in all workplaces where unions were recognised. Moreover since it was made the extent of trade union recognition has fallen further and it is therefore probable that access to safety representatives has also declined. Certainly, some support for this view is found in results from the Second European Survey on Working Conditions which indicates that only 25% British employees had access to a worker representative on health and safety[13].

The decline in the coverage of union safety representatives clearly reflects the dramatic fall that has occurred over the last two decades in the extent of union recognition. However, this decline, in turn, is itself the result of a number of other factors. These encompass the growth of employment in SMEs and smaller workplaces, the creation of more devolved management structures, the greater use of 'non-standard' forms of employment, and shifts of employment away from sectors where union organisation has traditionally been relatively strong (see chapter 2). They also include, the rise of anti-collectivistic management strategies, often associated with the concept of human resource management, and, until recently a hostile political environment marked, most notably by the passing of a range of anti-union legislation[14].

At the same time, notwithstanding these falls in union recognition and the coverage of union safety representatives, workers continue to see unions as playing an important role in protecting worker health and safety. Indeed this is true of non-union workers, as well as those who are union members[15].

Utilisation of safety representative functions

Existing evidence indicates that even where safety representative arrangements operate well, they tend to function at the standard implied in legislation and only rarely do they work at levels beyond this. It further suggests that in all too many cases their operation falls someway short of this standard. For example, a 1998 TUC survey found that only 24% of safety representatives were automatically consulted by management on a frequent basis and 21% were never consulted. This same study also revealed that the majority of representatives did not carry out formal inspections of the workplace as frequently as they are entitled to by Regulation 5 of the SRSC Regulations. Furthermore, other surveys suggest that a large percentage of safety representatives do not receive information on health and safety from their employer[16] in accordance with Regulation 7, and that it has become more difficult for them to obtain paid time off to carry out their functions[17].

More generally, the 1998 TUC survey found that less than 30% of safety representatives were satisfied with the extent of their involvement in drawing up risk assessment and 40% had not been involved at all in their preparation. This is despite the fact that risk assessment is central to the approach to health and safety management advocated by the Framework Directive and forms a fundamental part of a number of current regulatory packages, such as the MHSW regulations and those dealing with asbestos, display screen equipment, noise and the control of substances hazardous to health.

Safety representative training

The significance of both the quality and quantity of trade union training has emerged very clearly from European surveys as crucial to both the development and integration of health and safety representation at the workplace level[18]. It is also clear that trade union training for safety representatives in Britain has been one of the success stories in the development of worker representation in respect of health and safety since the coming into force of the HSW Act[19]. Nevertheless, the current situation with regard to the training of safety representatives is far from perfect. In particular:

- despite the large numbers of safety representatives receiving training, a significant proportion remain untrained[20]. The reasons for this are unclear, but it is commonly believed that they include an inability to obtain sufficient time-off from employers or the perception on the part of new representatives that they cannot afford the time away from their jobs;

- while the TUC approved courses which comprise the largest contribution to the training of safety representatives are generally seen as sound and well structured in terms of their methods, delivery and course content, since its inception the TUC programme has been subject to uncertain resourcing which has periodically occasioned changes in both the balance of its providers and and its funding. Such changes have led to periodical unevenness of provision, which may have contributed to some representatives finding it more difficult to obtain training locally; and

- considerable differences exist in the content and pedagogical approaches of the training provided via the TUC's programme, individual trade unions, joint employer/trade union initiatives, employers and commercial training. This in itself is not necessarily a problem. However, while TUC courses are accredited by the National Open College and, as a result of being largely provided by Colleges of Further or Higher Education, are also subject to the same external scrutiny and quality assessment as other aspects of FHE, this is for the most part not the case with those provided through other sources.

Enforcement

The provisions of the SRSC Regulations, with the exception of those relating to time-off, where their is a right of compliant to an employment tribunal, are enforced by HSE and local authority inspectors. However, from the outset the HSE has adopted a policy of avoiding inspector involvement in industrial relations issues by stressing that enforcement action should not be considered unless inspectors were satisfied that all voluntary methods of resolving disputes over the regulations had been tried. Presumably because of this, such action has hardly ever been taken.

At the same time the HSE does recommend that inspectors make contact with safety representatives when visiting a workplace. Unfortunately, the available evidence suggests that inspectors frequently do not make such contact. For example, a study of the activities of HSE field inspectors published in 1993 reported that even in workplaces with recognised trade union representatives, inspectors only make limited efforts to contact representatives during their visits and did not generally invite them to be present during inspections[21]. In the most recent survey of safety representatives conducted by the TUC nearly 40% of the respondents indicated that an inspector had never visited their workplace[22]. Taken together, this evidence therefore suggests that although safety representatives have legal rights to consult with inspectors and receive information from them, in practice few of them are able to make use of these rights.

HSCE Regulations

GIVEN the above findings on the coverage of union safety representatives, the advent of the 1996 HSCE Regulations was to be welcomed. However, this welcome must be a very qualified one. For, as
already noted, they introduced a much weaker regulatory framework
than that provided under the 1977 regulations. In particular, they do
not require employers to put in place any representative arrangements, but allow them instead to directly consult employees, accord
elected representatives fewer rights, and entrust employers with the
task of identifying training needs and meeting them.

These weaknesses are accentuated by two further problems. First,
elected RESs will not have access to the types of support and advice
provided by trade unions and secondly, may well operate in isolation
from broader systems of workplace representation

Existing research evidence on the factors that contribute to representative effectiveness adds weight to a pessimistic view of the likely
impact of representatives elected under the HSCE Regulations. For
example, both British and American studies have found safety committee to be more effective where management and employee members are well trained[23], while other research indicates that safety representative effectiveness is strongly influenced by[24]:

- the presence of a strong, centralised workplace trade union organisation;
- the integration of representatives into workplace union organisation;
- consultation between representatives and their constituents; and
- the provision of adequate information and training.

Leaving aside the crucial role of workplace union organisation identified above, it seems doubtful that the factors found to be conducive
to effective representation in the area of health and safety are likely
to be widely found in non-unionised environments. For example, the
research conducted on non-union safety representatives in the offshore oil industry mentioned earlier identified training to be one of
the most unsatisfactory areas of their experience[25]. In a similar vein,
evidence from other European countries suggests that even when
trade unions are not mentioned in legislation on worker representation, it is trade union representatives who benefit most from
training[26].

Options for reform

THE above review of the operation of the current legal framework for worker representation in respect of health and safety has

---

revealed that union safety representatives appointed under the SRSC operation exist in a minority of workplaces and that this coverage has been declining. It has also shown that the presence of such representatives varies between sectors and is lower in smaller workplaces, and further drawn attention to the fact that where they do exist, it is rare for the SRSC Regulations to be fully implemented. In addition, major doubts have been raised about the value of the HSCE Regulations as a mechanism for supporting the development of effective worker representation.

Given these conclusions, this section goes on to examine possible ways in which the structure and operation of the present legal framework could be improved. It does so by considering five, inter-related, issues: the role of safety representatives in health and safety management; their training; the issue of time off; the encouragement of representation in small enterprises; and the establishment of linkages with broader systems of worker representation.

Safety representatives and health and safety management

Safety representatives are intended to play an active role in the development and monitoring of health and safety arrangements at the workplace. Their current legal rights, however, are in a number of respects deficient with regard to providing support for this role.

A good case in point is the limited role that representatives are accorded in relation to preventive services. The model of preventive service advocated by the Framework Directive and increasingly adopted in other EU countries, is an integrated one in which occupational medicine, safety, hygiene, ergonomics and work psychology are all provided as a team-work approach towards the prevention of injury and ill-health and the improvement of working conditions and the working environment (see chapter 2). Essential to the operation of this strategy is its focus on risk assessment and on the involvement of workers and their representatives in the oversight of such services.

The 1998 TUC survey of safety representatives showed that there is still a long way to go to achieve this, both with regard to the integration of preventive services and in the involvement of worker representatives in the mechanisms for their accountability and control. In fact there is no evidence that this occurs to any significant extent even at the most minimal level of involvement that is represented by the requirements on employers to consult representatives on the matter of how "competent persons" are to be appointed or nominated for the purposes of the MSHW Regulations.

A further example of the way in which the current legal framework does not adequately provide for safety representatives to be centrally involved in the management of health and safety relates to their role in multi-employer workplaces, including those where sub-contracting arrangements operate. In some such workplaces well organised trade union safety representatives do in practice deal with the potential health and safety problems that can arise. For example, by negotiating agreements which extend representation to members no longer under the aegis of the central employer, or cover the nature of the contractual obligations imposed on subcontractors, including the provision to be made for health and safety consultation. Unfortunately, despite their obvious potential value, agreements of this type appear to be relatively uncommon. Part of the explanation for this seems likely to be that neither the SRSC Regulations or their general supporting ACOP lay down requirements or guidance on the role that representatives are entitled to play in workplaces where activities are undertaken by a number of different employers. For example, nothing is said about the need for a 'third party' employer to cooperate with safety representatives to enable them to carry out their functions. This is despite the fact that the duty on employers sharing a workplace under the MHSW regulations to cooperate with each other in order to enable them to fulfill their respective statutory duties would appear to indirectly require such cooperation.

Indeed, and more generally, while employers have obligations regarding consultation with representatives and are frequently exhorted to engage in such consultation in ACOPs and official guidance, no precise guidance is given on how this should be structured and facilitated. For example, what measures should be put in place to involve representatives in the planning and operation of auditing procedures, the design and carrying out of risk assessments, the adoption of new working methods and equipment, and the content and delivery of health and safety information and training?

Safety representative powers

A comparison of the rights and functions of worker representatives in Britain with those in other European countries reveals that there are a number of other ways in which they could be improved. For example, in many countries the right of worker representatives to call upon the aid of independent outside experts is more explicitly stated; the relationship of regulatory agency inspectors with them is the subject of more prescriptive provision; and in some European countries they are afforded more protection against victimisation.

In addition, in some countries, such as Sweden, representatives have the right to demand that work is stopped on processes which they believe to pose serious risks to health and safety – a right which is widely regarded as one of the most effective of the provisions on worker representation laid down in Swedish law[27]. Similarly, in some Australian States, including Victoria and Queensland, representatives have the right to issue Provisional Improvement Notices and as a result are effectively able to prevent the continuation dangerous work. Again, positive views about the effectiveness of this system are widespread[28].

In fact this Australian approach could be taken further and extend to the provision of rights to representatives and their unions to initiate private prosecutions for breaches of health and safety law and/or to bring complaints to an employment tribunal that their rights have been infringed. For example, the TUC has argued that the SRSC Regulations should give trade unions the right to bring complaints to a tribunal where they believe employers have demonstrated a sustained failure to consult. It has further proposed that this right should apply in respect of trade union members who work for employers that do not recognise unions. A similar role for Employment Tribunals could be developed in cases where employers refuse to release safety representatives to attend training courses and consistently fail to supply information requested by them under Regulation 7 Regulation of the SRSC Regulations. In this latter case access to information could be further enhanced through the development of a system in which safety representatives' rights to information could be extended by obliging suppliers to provide it when employers are unwilling or unable to co-operate.

Such rights of legal action could, in turn, be supported by two further developments. First, the adoption on the part of inspectors of a more rigorous approach to enforcing the statutory provisions on worker representation. Secondly, the placing by the HSE of greater emphasis on the need to make contact with representatives during workplace visits.

Safety representative training

Many of the studies on worker representation in health and safety confirm that training is a key support for effective representation. Further studies show that such representation improves health and safety performance. It follows from this that resources invested in training health and safety representatives are likely to produce significant benefits in both the reduction of injuries and ill-health and the economic costs associated with them. Such investment is therefore cost-effective. However, the history of support for the training of health and safety representatives is one that has been fraught with uncertainties concerning both the level and continuity of funding. It is clear that if representation is to fulfil its potential such uncertainties need to be removed and training adequately and continuously funded.

A better understanding of the link between training and workplace actions on health and safety could be achieved by following the Swedish example and commissioning research in this field[29]. The findings of this research could used to provide an informed approach to the future development of the content and methodology of training. A greater range of education and training provision could also be developed in which the issue of progression and accreditation is adequately addressed. While there are serious moves in this direction within the TUC Regional Education Programme and there are discussions taking place between some trade unions and organisations representing the health and safety professions, there is a need for a more systematic standardisation of the issues of education and training.

Other important questions in the training area centre on provision of training to non-union representatives. In particular, it seems clear that action is needed to both increase the access of such representatives to appropriate and adequate training, and to identify appropriate means of providing and funding this training.

One approach to dealing with these issues would be take action to link representation over health and safety to broader legally-based mechanisms of representation that apply equally to both unionised and non-unionised settings – an approach discussed in more detail below. Another, not necessarily mutually exclusive one, would be to utilise the sectoral insurance associations proposed in chapter 5 to both to develop and provide training to representatives in the much the same way that Work Environment Funds have been used to do so in Scandinavia.

Time-off and the role of safety representatives

If employers are to be encouraged to see the participation of workers' representatives more positively, then the language used to describe their activities needs to reflect a more positive approach. The term 'time-off' is not helpful in this respect. For safety representatives who undertake health and safety tasks are not 'having time off' but making an important contribution to improving health and safety standards. This last point is linked to another about language, namely the use of the term 'health and safety' itself.

As we have noted in chapter 2, work-related ill-health is currently dominated by conditions whose causes are multifactorial and which are as much influenced by the organisation, intensity and duration of work as they are by working conditions and the biological, physical and chemical hazards associated with them. This feature, when added to the influence of the precariousness of modern work, and the juxtaposition of work and domestic requirements, creates an environment which requires a more holistic approach to prevention than that captured within the traditional meaning of the term 'health and safety'. The need for such an approach is borne out by research findings which indicate that women face a different set of risks to their health and safety than men, in large part because of the inter-penetration of paid work and domestic responsibilities[30]. Its importance is also highlighted by recent survey results which show that safety representatives have been dealing with a rising number of complaints relating to occupational stress and also commonly handle problems associated with musculoskeletal disorders[31].

The need for such an approach has been recognised in Scandinavian countries for some time time. It is for this reason that they use the term 'work environment' in preference to 'health and safety'. It is also why the terminology used to describe worker representatives and their role has also sometimes changed. For example, in Denmark they are known as work environment representatives, while in Sweden the legislative requirements on worker representation refers to the "role of representatives in promoting employee participation in arrangements on the work environment and in activating work in this area". Surveys furthermore indicate that representatives perceive activating such work as their most important task[32].

Safety representatives and small enterprises

The special problems confronting worker representation in small enterprises need particular attention given the role it could play in improving their poor health and safety performance (see chapter 2) and the fact that they are resistant to many of the established means of achieving effective participative health and safety management. Indeed the question of how to overcome the obstacles which face the development of worker representation in such enterprises is one of the most important issues confronting current and future health and safety regulation.

Trade union regional health and safety representatives (also known as mobile, roving or territorial representatives) provide a potentially valuable means of addressing this issue. Certainly, other countries have considered that such representatives can play an important role. For example health and safety in small workplaces has been tackled with considerable success by regional safety delegates in Sweden[33], and in Norway there are long-standing legislative provisions for regional representatives in construction work. Similarly, in Spain regional worker representatives in health and safety are reported to be active in some regions and in Italy, as well as Spain, collective agreements exist, in the construction industry, for example, which establish district joint committees with equal trade union and employer membership that have the power to make site inspections. In addition, provisions exist in France and Belgium which provide trade unions with some rights in certain sectors of employment such as agriculture and construction, and in Greece legislation has provided for joint regional committees, some of which have been very active[34].

These findings lend support to the calls for legislative provisions for regional/mobile representatives which have been made by several trade unions. By creating such representatives, these provisions could go some way to dealing with the problem of representation in non-union workplaces by extending the right of trade union representatives to such employees. However, the realities of the present situation suggest that for regional/mobile representatives to have any chance of success certain support structures need to be put in place. In particular, the introduction of such a system of representation would seem to require:

- the agreement of the social partners and the regulatory authorities,
- adequate but cost effective resourcing,
- a clear and unambiguous definition of the task of the representative,
- a clear strategy for trade union support,
- inter-union co-operation and co-ordination with regard to the coverage and activities of such representatives; and
- special training and support for them.

In Norway and Sweden such training and support has been successfully provided through work environment funds. Such an approach could similarly be adopted here, either through funds of this type or via the system of sectoral insurance associations we have proposed in chapter 5.

Linkages with broader systems of worker representation

Legislation on worker representation in most European countries gives employers specific duties to facilitate and support the election of worker health and safety representatives within a broader legislative framework in which employers have obligations to honour workers' rights to representation. In contrast, in Britain a "two track" approach is utilised. Thus, on the one hand, recognised trade union have the power to appoint safety representatives and, on the other, employers who do not recognise unions are required to consult employees either directly or via elected representatives. Moreover if such representatives are elected, they have inferior rights to their union counterparts and have to carry out their functions in the likely absence of any broader mechanisms of representative support.

This approach is an untidy one that does not embody any sense of a planned or holistic strategy to the provision of legislative support for the representation of workers' interests. It is also one that, as we have seen, is unlikely to extend effective representation over health and safety issues to non-unionised workers – even, if the requirements on representation in the HSCE Regulations were to be made equivalent to those laid down in the 1977 regulatory regime. As a result any discussion of the future of worker representation on health and safety cannot be separated from the question of trade union recognition and worker representation in general.

Under the Employment Relations Act 1999 a new union recognition procedure is being put in place, albeit one that contains many limitations, and unions have acquired the right to represent workers in formal disciplinary and grievance hearings in workplaces where they do not have negotiating rights. This legislation may therefore act to stimulate trade union representation in the field of health and safety. It will, however, certainly not lead to the kind of framework for worker representation commonly found in other European Union countries. Thus, as the Prime Minister noted in the government's Fairness at Work white paper:

'*Even after the changes we propose, Britain will have the most lightly regulated labour market of any leading economy in the world*'[35]

If these reforms of employment law do not significantly improve the support for worker representation in health and safety, then more radical action appears to be needed. That is the introduction of a framework for linking systems of health and safety representation with broader representative mechanisms like the works council based systems found in other European countries. Such a move has in the past been strongly resisted by some trade unions, not least because of fears that measures of this type could be used to undermine union recognition and organisation. These concerns are clearly important but they must be weighed against the fact that there is no evidence that the wider remit of the legislative requirements in other European countries has negatively affected trade union influence in worker representation. Indeed there is quite a lot of evidence from these countries to suggest that it constitutes a platform on which trade union influence can build[36].

The way forward

STATUTORY provisions for the appointment and operation of trade union health and safety representatives have been remarkably effective in creating a system for worker representation in health and safety during a period when the wider determinants of employment relations were becoming increasingly unfavourable towards trade union activity. However, the restriction of the SRSC Regulations to recognised trade unions has increasingly constrained access to effective representation.

The workplaces in which the SRSC Regulations are known to work best – large workplaces with well-developed trade union organisation and a management sympathetic towards representative participation – have become less frequent since the measures were introduced. The result is increasing numbers of workers without access to representation and increasingly fewer workplaces in which the best conditions for the operation of the provisions are found. More recent requirements introduced to comply with the requirements of European directives come nowhere near addressing these problems in practice because they take no account of the factors that are known to support the effectiveness of worker representation in health and safety.

To improve this situation two types of change are necessary. The first involves modifications to the existing law and official guidance. The second encompasses actions to amend the wider context within which this law and guidance operates.

Modifications to law and guidance

The modifications we have in mind concern amendments to the existing statutory provisions and the development of an enhanced role for ACOPs in supporting these provisions. In the case of the former they include:

- an increased recourse for representatives and trade unions to Employment Tribunals in situations where employers demonstrate a sustained refusal to consult, deny representatives facilities to support their functions, or consistently refuse to supply statutory health and safety information to health and safety representatives;
- measures to allow trade unions to represent members, whether or not they work for an employer who recognises them for the purposes of collective bargaining;
- action to provide for mobile health and safety representatives for

small firms. Initially such measures could be introduced in sectors of employment in which there is a demonstrable case to support their likely effectiveness with a view to further extension to other sectors at later dates;

- amendments to other health and safety provisions to ensure that they impose specific obligations on employers' obligations to facilitate and undertake consultation with representatives;
- extension of the rights of worker representatives to issue 'provisional improvement notices' where they believe there to be a serious infringement of health and safety standards and to 'stop the job' where they believe there is an imminent and serious risk to health or safety;
- stronger measures to ensure consultation of health and safety representatives by employers when they are deciding on the type of preventive services required and to ensure a role for representatives in the oversight of the activities of such services;
- more onerous obligations on employers to release representatives for training and to make provision for covering their absence, and a similar strengthening of requirements on the release of representatives to carry out their health and safety functions at the workplace;
- the introduction of a right for safety representatives, as representatives of users, to require information from suppliers on safe and healthy use of articles and substances; and
- the creation of compatibility between the rights accorded to representatives under the SRSC and HSCE Regulations and a reduction of the scope for employers to consult directly with employees under the HSCE Regulations as an alternative to making arrangements for worker representation.

With regard to ACOPs, which hitherto have been under-utilised in the regulation of worker representation in health and safety, we further propose that these be used to:

- set standards of competence for health and safety representatives;
- provide more support for trade union training through setting training quality standards that are linked to competence;
- provide systems for the accreditation and certification of representative training provision;
- deal with issues concerning the recognition and operation of representatives in multi-employer worksites, including those where subcontracting is undertaken;
- oblige inspectors of regulatory agencies to consult with representatives;
- provide more structured and detailed requirements concerning

employers' obligations to facilitate the election of health and safety representatives and the creation of joint safety committees;

- improve the practical operation of measures to protect health and safety representatives from victimisation by employers; and
- make clear that the role of representatives extends to include the protection of workers from psycho-social harm.

The broader regulatory context

The above changes, however desirable, will not provide a framework of law within which all workers could reasonably expect to have access to effective representation on health and safety. For this reason the new legislative provisions on union recognition and representation, are to be warmly welcomed. However, these provisions appear unlikely to be sufficient either. Consequently, we further believe that there is a need to create a general legal framework for worker representation, along the lines of the works council systems used in other European countries, in which the specific obligations on health and safety can be located.

A move in this direction would undoubtedly meet strong resistance. The European Commission has, however, recently proposed a directive on national information and consultation rules[37]. In its current form this would require all undertakings with at least 50 employees to inform and consult employee representatives about a range of business, employment and work organisation issues. Its adoption could therefore require the UK to introduce representative systems akin to the works council ones used elsewhere in Europe, and therefore open up the possibility of creating the type of linkage between health and safety and more general representation, advocated above. We believe that it is only with such a system of general representation rights that provisions for non-trade union health and safety representatives would be likely to stand any chance of being effective. If such general provisions were introduced, then we would further recommend that measures to create compatibility between rights accorded to representatives under the SRSC and HSCE Regulations should be introduced. Under these circumstances it might also be desirable to introduce legislative measures requiring employers to make arrangements for joint consultative committees for health and safety such as is the case in some other European countries.

Unfortunately, at present the UK and German governments have voiced concerns about the directive and it is therefore far from clear whether it will be eventually adopted. Were it to be adopted, careful thought would need to be given to how it could be transposed in a way that would facilitate and develop trade union support for worker representation in health and safety since, ultimately, there is no substitute for such support. Indeed, the encouragement of this support should, in our view, form a central consideration in the design of any broader mechanism of worker representation of this type.

It also needs to be recognised that the currently proposed directive would still not deal with worker representation in very small undertakings. As a result it would not represent a substitute for the system of regional/mobile safety representatives that we have proposed. In addition, and more generally, it would not avoid the need for two other developments that we have identified as desirable. First, the adoption by HSE and local authority inspectors of a more rigorous approach to the enforcement of representational rights and within this, a greater recognition of the need for representatives to be supported to adopt a more "holistic" role in respect of the protection of worker health and safety. Secondly, the provision, either through sectoral insurance associations or a work environment fund, of resources to support both the proposed system of mobile safety representatives and the more general, expansion of worker representation and associated training.

Conclusion

THIS chapter has provided a critical evaluation of the present statutory requirements on worker representation in respect of health and safety laid down under the SRSC and HSCE Regulations. The evaluation has revealed a number of weaknesses in both the structure and operation of this legislative framework.

In the case of the SRSC Regulations the chapter has drawn attention to the fact that the coverage of representatives appointed under the former regulations has been declining with the result that most workers, and particularly those in small workplaces, are not covered by them. It has also shown that where such representatives have been appointed, it is relatively rare for them to make full use of their legal powers and that employers frequently do not comply with either the latter or spirit of the law. This latter failing has, in turn, been noted to have been compounded by the failure of inspectors to adequately enforce the 1997 regulations.

As regards the HSCE Regulations, a number of fundamental weaknesses in their provisions have been highlighted. Notable among these being, the scope they give employers to avoid the establishment of representative systems and the limited powers that they make available to representatives who are elected under them. A variety of problems have also been identified with regard to employer awareness of and compliance with, the regulations. In addition, doubts have been expressed about the likely effectiveness of non-union representation that is divorced from adequate training and other forms of support.

A range of proposals have been put forward to address the above problems. These fall under two broad headings. First, modifications to current law, along with the provision of an enhanced role for ACOPs. Secondly, the establishment of a broader framework of worker representation within which representative systems for health and safety can be located.

In the former area the changes proposed include, the provision of new rights to both representatives and unions to bring complaints before an employment tribunal; the establishment of a system of mobile safety representatives aimed at enhancing representation in small workplaces; and the provision of enhanced powers to representatives, including rights concerning the overseeing of preventive services, the issuing of provisional improvement notices and the stopping of dangerous work. In the latter it is suggested that health and safety representation be integrated into works council style arrangements and that this move be supported by the adoption on the part of inspectors of a more rigorous approach to the enforcement of representative rights.

Summary of key points

Worker representation

- increased rights to safety representatives and trade unions to enforce statutory provisions on worker representation;
- introduction of measures to allow trade unions to represent members, whether or not they work for an employer who recognises them for the purposes of collective bargaining;
- action to establish systems of mobile safety representatives covering small firms;
- provision to safety representative of powers to issue 'provisional improvement notices' where they believe there to be a serious infringement of health and safety standards and to 'stop the job' where they believe there is a serious and imminent risk to workers;
- introduction of legal rights to safety representatives regarding the establishment, role and operation of occupational health and safety services;
- imposition of more onerous obligations on employers to provide safety representatives with 'health and safety' time to undergo training and carry out their statutory functions;
- introduction of a right for safety representatives to require information from suppliers of articles and substances;
- adoption by HSE and local authority inspectors of a more rigorous approach to the enforcement of representational rights and within this, the according of greater recognition to the need for safety representatives to adopt a more "holistic" role in respect of the protection of worker health and safety; and
- establishment of a general legal framework for worker representation (along the lines of the works council systems used within other European countries) to act as a "fall back" position in situations where trade unions are not recognised to ensure that health and safety representation is located and supported by broader mechanisms of worker representation.

Notes

1 J. Williams, *Accidents and Ill Health at Work*, 1960, Staples Press.
2 see D.R. Walters, "Trade unions and the effectiveness of worker representation in health and safety in Britain", *International Journal of Health Services*, 26(4), 1996, 625- 641, Baywood; E. Tucker, "Worker Participation in Health and Safety Regulation: Lessons from Sweden" *Studies in Political Economy*, 37, 1992; N. Dedobbeleer, F. Champagne and P. German, 'Safety performance among Union and Nonunion Workers in the Construction Industry', *Journal of Occupational Medicine*, 32(11), 1990, 1099-1103; L. Grunberg, 'The Effects of the Social Relations of Production on Productivity and Workers' Safety', *International Journal of Health Services*, 13(4), 1983, 621-634; M. Quinlan, 'The industrial relations of occupational health and safety' in M. Quinlan (ed), *Work and Health, the origins, management and regulation of occupational illness*, Macmillan. 1993, 126-169; D. Biggins, M. Phillips, and P. O'Sullivan, 'Benefits of worker participation in health and safety', *Labour and Industry*, 4(1), 1991, 138-59; P. Warren-Langford, D. Biggins and M. Phillips, 'Union participation in occupational health and safety in Western Australia', *Journal of Industrial Relations*, 35(4), 1993, 585-606; DR Walters and S. Gourlay, *Statutory Employee Involvement in Health and Safety at the Workplace: A Report of the Implementation and Effectiveness of the Safety Representatives and Safety Committees Regulations 1977*, HSE Contract Research Report No. 20/1990, 1990, HMSO; B. Reilly, P. Paci and P. Holl, "Unions Safety Committees and Workplace Injuries", *British Journal of Industrial Relations*, 33(2), 1995; DR Walters, "Health and Safety and Trade Union Workplace Organization: A case study in the printing industry", Industrial Relations Journal, 18 (1), 40-49; and R. Patterson and DR Walters, "Health and Safety in Hotels and Catering" in D. Byrne, *Waiting for Change?*, 1986, Low Pay Unit.
3 See T. Nichols, The Sociology of Industrial Injury, 1997, Mansell; Reilly et al, op cit; and P. Beaumont and R. Harris, 'Health and safety in union and non-union establishments', 23(7), 1993, *Occupational Health and Safety.*
4 Lord Robens, *Safety and Health at Work: Report of the Committee 1970-72*, Cmnd 5034, 1972, para 70.
5 See *Safety Representatives and Safety Committees*, 3rd edition, 1996, HSE.
6 See "Victimisation on health and safety grounds", *Industrial Relations Law Bulletin*, 546, June 1996, 2-7.
7 *EC Commission v United Kingdom:* C-383/92 [1994], IRLR 412; and *EC Commission v United Kingdom:* C-382/92 [1994], IRLR 392.
8 See P. James and D. Walters, 'Non-union rights of involvement: the case of health and safety at work', *Industrial Law Journal*, 26, 1997, 35-50.
9 M. Spaven and C. Wright, *The Effectiveness of Offshore Safety Representatives and Safety Committees: A Report to the HSE*, 1993, HSE. Also see C. Woolfson, J. Foster and M. Beck, *Paying the Piper: Capital and Labour in Britain's Offshore Oil Industry*, 1996, Mansell.
10 'Safely appointed', *Employment Gazette*, February 1981, 55-58.
11 Walters and Gourlay, 1990, op cit.
12 Trades Union Congress, *The future of workplace safety representatives: interim report of the TUC common action priority team on safety representatives*, March 1995, TUC.

13 (25) European Foundation for Improvement of Living and Working Conditions, *Second European Survey of the Working Environment,* 1997, Office for Official Publications of the European Communities.

14 See generally J. Waddington and C. Whitson, 'Trade Unions: Growth, Structure and Policy' in P. Edwards (ed), *Industrial Relations: Theory and Practice in Britain,* 1995, Blackwell.

15 See eg J. Monks, *Safety and Justice: What Unions can give to the giving society,* 1997, Trades Union Congress.

16 Walters and Gourlay, 1990, op cit.

17 P. Kirby, *TUC Survey of Safety Reps,* 1998, Trades Union Congress.

18 A. Raulier and D.R. Walters, *Trade Union Training in Health and Safety: A Survey of European Practice in Training for Worker Representatives,* 1995, Trade Union Technical Bureau, Brussels.

19 DR Walters, "Trade Unions and the Training of Health and safety Representatives in Europe", *Employee Relations,* 18(6).

20 Raulier and Walters, 1995, op cit.

21 B. Hutter, "Regulating Employers and Employees: Health and Safety in the Workplace", *Journal of Law and Society,* 20(4), 1993, 452-470.

22 P. Kirby, *TUC survey of safety reps,* 1998, Trades Union Congress. See also the results of a previous TUC survey: "Congress turns to violence as safety representatives focus on stress and overwork", *Health and Safety Information Bulletin,* October 1996, 3.

23 P. Beaumont, J. Coyle, J. Leopold and T. Schuller, *The Determinants of Effective Joint Health and Safety Committees,* 1982, Centre for Research into Industrial Democracy and Participation, University of Glasgow, (Report to ERSC); and T. Kochan, L. Dyer, and D. Lipsky, *The Effectiveness of Union-Management Safety and Health Committees,* 1977, W.E. Upjon Institute for Employment Research.

24 Walters and Gourlay, 1990, op cit.

25 Spaven and Wright, 1993, op cit.

26 D.R. Walters, "Trade unions and the training of health and safety representatives in Europe", *Employee Relations,* 18(6), 1998.

27 D.R. Walters, A. Dalton and D. Gee, *Worker Representation on Health and Safety in Europe,* 1993, European Trade Union Technical Bureau for Health and Safety, Brussels.

28 C. Dyer, "Underpinning Safety Reps: Budgets or Bureaucracy?", *Health and Safety Bulletin,* 274, December 1998, 17-23

29 T. Erasmie and H. Bonnevier, Arbetsmiljoutbildning, Mal - Insats - Effekt, Utvardering av Utbildningsverksamhet som Stods av Arbetmiljofonden, 1988 University of Linkoping; and L. Holmstrand, L.S. Solveborn and A. Englund, A., *Utvardering av den Fackliga Funkionsutbildningen,* 1993, Uppsala University.

30 See K. Kauppinen and I. Kandolin, Gender and Working Conditions in the European Union, 1997, European Foundation for the Improvement of Living and Working Conditions; and K. Messing, 'Les Fesses de femmes et la sante au travail', Cahiers du Feminisme, 58, 1991, 12-13.

31 Kirby, 1998, op cit.

32 Frick and Walters, forthcoming, op cit.

33 K. Frick and D.R. Walters, "Regional safety representatives: a Swedish

approach to worker representation on health and safety in small enterprises", International Labour Review (forthcoming); and DR Walters, "Lessons from Sweden, the Swedish regional health and safety representatives and health and safety in small enterprises", *Health and Safety Bulletin,* No. 268, 1998.

34 66.See, for example, reports presented by national trade union officials at a TUTB/CISL seminar, Rome, June 1998, TUTB Brussels.

35 *Fairness at Work,* Department of Trade and Industry White Paper, The Stationery Office, CM 3968, 1998

36 See eg. D.R. Walters and R.J. Freeman, *Employee Representation in Health and Safety at the Workplace: A Comparative Study in Five European Countries,* 1992, Report EUR 13508 EN,992, Commission of the European Communities

37 See "European Parliament backs draft EU consultation directive", *European Works Council Bulletin,* 21, May/June 1999, 1-2.

Chapter 5

Amelioration of work-related harm

EACH year it is estimated that around 25,000 people leave employment as a result of work-related injury and illness.[1] Available figures further suggest that such injury and ill health results in the loss of over 25 million working days each year and that during a further 300 million days workers experience limitations on their daily activities which stem from work-related illnesses[2].

These figures, when considered in conjunction with those provided in chapter 2 on the scale of deaths, injuries and ill health caused by work, point to the fact that work activities continue to impose enormous costs on both workers and their families via loss of income, pain and suffering, and disruption of social and domestic life. They further point to the fact that this harm imposes a heavy burden on the taxpayer through medical treatment provided by the National Health Service and the payment of social security benefits. Indeed HSE estimates suggest that in 1990 work-related injuries and illness cost the taxpayer between £0.2 and £0.4 billion in medical treatment and around £58 million in Department of Social Security administration costs[3].

In effect therefore the taxpayer and workers and their families bear a substantial proportion of the costs that arise as a result of the failure of employers to protect adequately the health and safety of workers. This is surely undesirable. For, insofar as employers do not bear the full consequences of the harm they inflict on workers, they are receiving a subsidy that reduces their economic incentive reduce and avoid work injury and illness.

This chapter examines how this situation can be changed. Initially it examines what employers currently do to ameliorate work-related harm through the provision of financial support and rehabilitation services aimed at assisting workers to return to work and remain in employment. It then considers the adequacy of these arrangements and draws on international experience to identify how they can be improved.

Employer provided financial support

EMPLOYERS currently provide financial support to those suffering work-related injury and ill health through three main means: occupational sick pay; occupational pensions; and employers' liability insurance. Each of these sources of support are, however, very partial in terms of the support they provide.

Sick pay. Beyond the requirement to pay statutory sick pay (SSP) of £57.50 per week for a period of 28 weeks to employees who earn above the national insurance lower earnings limit, employers have complete discretion as to the sick pay arrangements they put in place. As a result, while some workers are covered by relatively generous arrangements, for example, 104 weeks on full-pay, others receive much less and indeed may receive nothing more than SSP. For example, a Confederation of British Industry (CBI) survey on managing absence found that 11% of responding organisations did not have an occupational sick pay scheme[4], while a Law Commission study of the experiences of a sample of compensated accident victims found that a third of those who had returned to their pre-accident job had received full pay during their absence, a quarter had not received any pay at all and the remainder had either received only part-pay or a combination of full and part-pay[5].

Moreover where an employer does have a sick pay scheme, it frequently will not extend to cover temporary workers. A graphic illustration of this is provided by a study of contract workers on two offshore oil platforms. Thus this found that if such workers, who form a large component of the offshore workforce, were sent home because of an illness or injury, they received only a small retainer from their employer and as a result immediately lost a large proportion of their income[6].

Pensions. It is similarly left to employers to decide not only whether to provide an occupational pension scheme, but also the nature of the scheme to be made available and the conditions that determine employee access to it. The net result is that in 1995 only 58% of men and 55% of women in full-time employment were members of such schemes and the corresponding figures for part-timers were even lower[7]. Furthermore, not all of these schemes were of the final salary type and hence potentially enabled employees to retire early on ill health grounds and receive credit not only for accrued service but for the future service which would have been completed had they continued in service until normal retirement age. Indeed there is evidence that schemes of this type are becoming increasingly uncommon as employers elect to move to the use of money purchase schemes[8].

Some employers do admittedly provide Permanent Health Insurance (PHI) under which employees receive regular payments which normally provide them, in conjunction with state benefits, with close to full earnings, during periods when they are unable to work, either fully or partially, up to normal retirement age. However, the available evidence indicates that only a minority of employers take out such insurance, and where they do, it normally only covers certain grades of more senior staff[9].

Employers' liability insurance. As regards employers liability insurance, this does generally ensure, providing that employers comply with their statutory obligation to have such insurance[10], that employees are able to receive any compensation awarded as a result of personal injury litigation. It also provides an important and valuable means of financial support. Indeed, as a result of cuts to the IIS, a policy of only uprating the benefits provided under it by reference to price rather than earnings inflation, and the Department of Social Security's policy of clawing back benefits paid to those compensated through employers' liability insurance, payments by insurers now exceed those made under the state scheme[11].

At the same time the current system of compulsory employers' liability insurance does have a number of weaknesses. For example, it does not extend to cover non-employees, doubts exist as to whether the minimum level of required insurance cover is sufficient, and no "guarantee fund" exists to provide compensation in cases where employers have failed to comply with their legal obligation to insure[12]. In addition, the role of such insurance is limited by the fact that personal injury litigation provides compensation to only a small proportion of those harmed as a result of their work activities. Thus, one study found that only a quarter of work accident victims consulted a solicitor and just one in five eventually obtained damages, while the Pearson committee found that just 10.5% of those suffering "reportable" injuries received tort compensation[13]. Furthermore, it seems likely that this situation will worsen as a result of the government's decision to withdraw legal aid from personal injury claims and introduce a conditional fees arrangement under which solicitors agree to undertake cases on the basis of receiving a proportion of any compensation awarded.

Finally, employers' liability premiums are in most cases determined solely by reference to the type of activities undertaken. As a result they are not generally influenced by the health and safety performance of employers and hence do not provide them with a clear incentive to reduce levels of work-related injury and ill health.

More generally, the current system of personal injury litigation has a number of weaknesses. First, while it can provide workers with substantial damages and access to compensation for conditions not covered by the Industrial Injuries Scheme (IIS – see below), courts are precluded from awarding punitive damages where employers have recklessly exposed workers to danger. Secondly, it is at present not possible to initiate actions in repsect of breaches of the Management of Health and Safety at Work (MHSW) Regulations and the general duties of the Health and Safety at Work (HSW) Act. Thirdly, such litigation is of little value to workers who suffer from ill health the origins of which is multifactorial and those who have conditions that are the outcome of chronic incremental damage incurred through employment with a variety of employers – a common situation among construction workers.

Employer provided rehabilitation

THE term rehabilitation can be seen to encompass two main elements. First, medical treatment aimed at maximising recovery from physical or mental illness. Secondly, the provision of vocational services, such as functional evaluations, training and work adaptions, intended to enable workers to retain or obtain employment. Rehabilitation can therefore require contributions from a number of different types of specialist, for example, doctors, nurses, physiotherapists, occupational therapists, psychologists and ergonomists.

Employers can potentially provide rehabilitation via a number of avenues – private medical insurance, PHI cover, since most insurers underwriting this type of policy provide access to rehabilitation, in-house staff or outside providers. The existing evidence, however, suggests that none of these avenues are widely used. Fewer than 2,000 employers, for example, make private medical treatment available to their staff through corporate insurance policies, according to figures published by the Association of British Insurers, and these policies are in most cases restricted to particular categories of managerial personnel. In a similar vein the HSE survey of occupational health provision mentioned earlier not only found that there was access to occupational health professionals in just 8% of private sector workplaces, but that these professionals mainly comprised of doctors and nurses, and, less frequently, hygienists. It further found that only in a small minority of cases did their role extend to include the treatment of injury and illness[14].

Against this background, it is perhaps not surprising that employers have been found to commonly do little to investigate whether anything can be done to facilitate the return to work of ill and injured workers. For example, in a 1993 study of disabled workers who had both received invalidity benefit during the previous year and returned to work, no less than 77% of those surveyed stated that their employer had not provided them with any assistance[15]. It would appear therefore that the approach adopted by many employers is to accept the absence of employees for a certain period of time and then consider whether their employment should be terminated. In effect therefore they adopt a policy of doing little or nothing and then pass the "problem" on to the employee and the state (through the provision of social security benefits and on-going medical treatment).

How far this situation is in the process of changing as a result of the coming into force of the Disability Discrimination Act and in particular, its requirements relating to the provision of reasonable accommodations is unclear. However, the evidence which is available is far from reassuring. Thus, one survey covering 77 organisations found that only a small number of them provided access to occupational/physical therapy or rehabilitation, while another found that over a quarter of disabled people who had left their jobs as a result of their disability felt that they could have stayed in work had necessary workplace adaptations been made[16].

This lack of activity is highly disturbing given that in 1995 43,000 workers had been off work for over six months due to work-related sickness, and that many of these were suffering from musculoskeletal disorders, and stress, depression or anxiety – conditions that are frequently amenable to rehabilitative interventions[17]. It is also worrying given that survey evidence suggests that over a quarter of those suffering from a work-related illness in 1995 had been forced to change their job as a result of it[18], and that examples exist which demonstrate that much can do much to minimise employee absence arising from such illness. For example, a physiotherapy service set up at Rover's Longbridge plant to assist workers suffering from musculoskeletal disorders is reported to have made a "noticeable dent" in the plant's sickness absence rate[19].

The case for a new approach

THE above evidence of present employer-based arrangements relating to rehabilitation and compensation reveals a complex and highly differentiated situation. Some, but a lucky few, workers have access to occupational sick pay, private medical treatment, PHI cover, and early retirement through "final salary" occupational pension schemes. Others have access to some, but not all of these benefits, most notably sick pay, while yet others, including presumably many of the growing army of temporary and self-employed workers, have to rely solely on SSP, state benefits and rehabilitation through the NHS and other government agencies. Even this, however, doesn't capture fully the highly differentiated nature of the present arrangements. For it takes no account of the marked differences that exist in occupational sick pay and pension schemes and the fact that only a small proportion of those injured or made ill through their work succeed in obtaining damages through personal injury litigation.

This situation is clearly inequitable, particularly when it is borne in mind that it is the workers most likely to be harmed by their work who are frequently among those in the least favourable position. It is also unacceptable. For it cannot be right that workers whose earning potential is reduced, whether temporarily or permanently, through no fault of their own should suffer financial loss.

These failings in employer compensation and rehabilitation arrangements are moreover compounded by weaknesses in the existing state provision in respect of both compensation and rehabilitation[20]. In the case of the former the only state provided support provided specifically in respect of work-related injury and disease is the Industrial Injuries Disablement Benefit (IIDB) provided under the IIS. This benefit, which is not means-tested and is provided on a no-fault basis after 15 weeks of disablement, is relatively generous compared with other social security benefits. It is nevertheless very low. Thus, the maximum benefit payable for 100% disablement is £108.10 per week for those over 18 or under 18 with dependents – a figure which goes down to £66.20 for 18 year olds without dependents.

In addition, access to IIDB is restricted in three important respects. First, in terms of work-related illness, it is only available in respect of certain "prescribed diseases". Secondly, workers in most cases only quality to receive the benefit if the extent of their disability is assessed at 14% or more. Thirdly, it is not available to self-employed workers. These qualifying criteria, in combination with a lack of awareness among workers of their rights to claim IIDB, mean that most work-related harm is not compensated under the IIS – a situation illustrated by the fact that only around 2,500 successful claims are made each year. In particular, only rarely will workers suffering from musculoskeletal disorders and stress-related conditions, which as was noted in chapter 2, are the most common forms of work-related illness, qualify to receive IIDB.

As a result many victims of work-related ill health are forced to rely on other, less generous, income- or disability-related state benefits. The potentially most valuable of these, Incapacity Benefit is, however, only available to those who have made the necessary national insurance contributions. In addition, continued receipt of it after 28 weeks is dependent on claimants passing an "All-Work Test", a test, which as its name implies, requires workers to demonstrate that they are unable to undertake work of any kind. Furthermore, under current government proposals the benefit will in future become means tested.

As regards state provided rehabilitation, the National Health Service (NHS) of course provides universal access to medical treatment through both primary and secondary care. Unfortunately, workers often experience long delays in receiving the treatment they need, during which time they may be experiencing financial loss and the threat of losing their employment. This problem is, in turn, accentuated by the fact that there is a marked absence of occupational health expertise within the NHS. Thus, only limited occupational health training is provided by medical schools, many GPs have chosen not to study the subject as part of their continuing medical education, and few primary health care teams have any specialist expertise in occupational health. As a result there are virtually no clinical occupational health specialists employed in hospitals or within NHS regions.

It is therefore no surprise that support groups for occupational disease sufferers frequently complain about the difficulties they face in getting their diseases first recognised and then appropriately treated. A case in point is a recent follow-up by the North Derbyshire Trade Union Safety Committee of workers exposed to the carcinogen vinyl chloride monomer (VCM). Thus this found that while many of the workers contacted had symptoms consistent with the long-term effects of VCM exposure, none had been followed up and there was no knowledge of the effects of VCM among the doctors they encountered[21].

The NHS does admittedly also provide a range of other services relevant to the rehabilitation of ill and injured workers, including specialist help for people with sensory impairments, assistance through community mental health teams, and the work of physiotherapists and occupational therapists. The latter forms of support are, however, often very limited. For example, total membership of the Chartered Society of Physiotherapy currently stands at just over 30,000, a proportion of whom work in the private sector and very few of whom have specialist occupational health expertise. It should also be noted that the rehabilitation services so provided are focused on improving functioning and living skills and are therefore only indirectly concerned with current and future employment.

The above NHS provision is supported by a variety of schemes run by the Department for Education and Employment (DfEE) which both assist workers to remain employed and offer help to those wishing to re-enter employment. These include, the work of Placement Assessment and Counselling Teams (PACTs) aimed at those who are almost ready to (re-)enter employment, the provision of vocational training through Training and Enterprise Councils and other bodies, and the Access to work scheme which provides various forms of financial and other support to disabled people in employment. In addition, local authorities may play a role at the local level in determining employment support and rehabilitation for disabled workers through their community care programmes. However, as a recent study noted, these various employment support and rehabilitation services are very piecemeal and un-coordinated with the result that it is very difficult for any one organisation to take overall responsibility for the welfare of a particular individual[22]. This is despite the fact that effective "case management" is widely recognised as an important determinant of successful rehabilitation[23].

Reforming the present system

A variety of proposals have been put forward to overcome the above weaknesses in current rehabilitation and compensation arrangements, including the lack of financial incentives they provide to encourage employers to prevent the occurrence of work-related harm. In particular, the following reforms have been suggested:

i) establishing a system under which the NHS reclaims the costs it incurs in treating the victims of work-related harm from employers;

ii) reforming the IIS to introduce differential contributions or premiums for either individual employers or for different industries;

iii) expanding the list of diseases prescribed under the IIS to encompass all those contained in the corresponding European list and also introduce a system under workers can seek to prove that their condition is work-related;

iii) introducing a greater degree of performance-rating into the setting of employers' liability insurance premiums; and

iv) requiring employers' liability insurers to take action to rehabilitate injured and ill workers.

Each of these reforms have attractions. However, they all also have limitations.

The option of allowing the NHS to reclaim the costs of treatment would, on practical grounds, almost certainly have to be restricted to cases of workplace injury which had been the subject of successful personal injury litigation. There must also be doubts about the feasibility of introducing differential contributions under the IIS, not least because of the relatively small number of claims made, while the existing evidence in those countries where "individual proof" systems exist, indicates that few workers succeed in demonstrating the work-relatedness of their condition[24].

As regards reforming the present system of employers' liability insurance to provide a greater degree of performance-rating, it needs to be recognised that a move in this direction would face major difficulties. First, the problems associated with using claims experience to determine the premiums of smaller employers who, statistically, would only rarely be the subject of personal injury claims. Secondly, the likely inability of insurers, given the precarious financial position of the employers' liability market, to either engage in a substantial degree of performance-rating or to finance a more sophisticated system of evaluating health and safety performance through workplace inspections[25].

It is true nonetheless that a number of insurers are already taking steps to do something in the rehabilitation area as a means of assisting workers to return to work more speedily and thereby reducing the size of subsequent compensation claims. This action is clearly to be welcomed. At the same time it remains unclear how far insurers will be willing to go down this road in respect of claims where the issue of employer fault, and hence likely liability, is unclear. Given this, there seem grounds for not solely relying on voluntary action on the part of insurers. One possible way of overcoming this problem would be for the Lord Chancellor to approve a pre-action protocol under which insurers would be required to offer early rehabilitation to claimants. The fact nevertheless remains that there would have to be a claim before access to rehabilitation could be obtained. It is also hard to believe that the insurance industry would willingly embrace a system whereby any claim, no matter what its apparent strength, would create an entitlement to potentially costly rehabilitation.

These problems therefore suggest that essentially tinkering with the present system is unlikely to overcome the problems that exist with regard to the present arrangements relating to the compensation and rehabilitation of ill and injured workers. In other words they suggest that something more radical needs to be done.

Other national systems

COMPENSATION and rehabilitation arrangements relating to work-related harm vary considerably between countries. Here brief, and hopefully not misleading, descriptions are provided of the key features of those in place in five countries – Australia – New South Wales, Germany, the Netherlands, Sweden and the United States of America (USA). These have been chosen on the grounds that between them they highlight some of the main differences in national approaches to the provision of compensation and rehabilitation by employers.

Australia – New South Wales

In Australia each state has its own workers' compensation scheme which provides compensation for work-related injuries and illnesses on a no-fault basis. These schemes differ significantly in terms of the way in which they are administered, the benefit levels provided, the role played by common law damages and the provision made for worker rehabilitation.

The New South Wales scheme is governed by the Workers Compensation Act 1987[26]. Under this workers who suffer a personal injury (a term which includes work-related diseases) arising out of or in the course of their employment are entitled to claim compensation, providing that employment was a substantial contributing factor to the condition concerned. However, workers whose injury exceeds one of a specified number of thresholds can opt to forgo payments under the scheme and instead seek civil compensation.

During the first 26 weeks of absence the benefits provided equate with the current weekly wage, subject to a maximum of $1,119.30 (£466.38). After this the benefit is reduced to 90% of earnings or $263.30 (£109.71), whichever is the lower, with additional payments being made in respect of a dependent spouse (£28.91) and children. However once the period of absence exceeds 104 weeks this payment may be discontinued where the worker does not meet the criteria of serious ongoing capacity and has not made reasonable attempts to return to work. In addition, claimants are entitled to up to $50,000 (£20,833) for medical and hospital treatment, although in certain circumstances this can be increased, and may also qualify for a lump sum payment of $100,000 (£41,667) plus $50,000 (£20,833) compensation for pain and suffering. In the event of a claimant's death their survivors are entitled to a death benefit of $237,150 (£98,812) plus a weekly benefit of $74.50 (£31.04) for each dependent child.

The above compensation is funded by a levy on employers –

although employers with more than 1,000 employees can seek to self-insure. In July 1998 this levy averaged 2.8%. However, this average figure encompassed different rates, ranging from 0.4% for medical practices to 10.36% for steel castings, for different industrial sectors. In addition, levies are experience rated, with the highest experience rating being set at 24% and lowest at around 0.2%.

Employers, by virtue of the Industrial Relations Act, cannot lawfully dismiss an injured employee for a period of 26 weeks. They are also obliged to establish a workplace rehabilitation programme to assist their injured employees to return to work. In addition, where more than 20 people are employed, a full-time or part-time, rehabilitation coordinator must be appointed to liaise with key personnel such as the worker's supervisor and treating doctor, and must develop written return-to-work programmes for workers who have been incapacitated for more than 12 weeks[27].

Germany

In Germany a system of 94 accident insurance institutions, the Berufsgenossenschaften (BGs), form an integral part of the country's social security system[28]. These associations, which are jointly governed by representatives of employers and workers, have three main statutory duties. First the prevention of accidents at work, a role which includes the provision of safety training to both workers and safety personnel. Secondly, the medical, vocational and social rehabilitation of victims of work-related accidents and disease. Thirdly, the payment of compensation to the victims and their survivors.

The associations are financed by employer payroll levies which are based on risk factors applicable to the constituent trade group to which they are assigned. However, allowance may be made for a firm's safety performance by reducing the figure by up to 50% for good performance or increasing it by up to 80% for bad.

In terms of prevention BGs are empowered to issue regulations that, once agreed by the Ministry of Labour, have legal force covering: the equipment, arrangements and measures which have to be provided by the employer to ensure a safe and healthy working environment; the conduct of employees; the medical examinations to be carried out before employment involving exposure to abnormal accident or health hazards; and the measures employers must take to fulfil their statutory health and safety duties. Compliance with these regulations is checked by inspectors, who operate in parallel with Lander appointed inspectors and are also heavily involved in the provision of advice to employers.

With regard to compensation, a variety of different types of benefits are provided to insured workers in respect of work accidents (including work-related driving accidents), occupational diseases listed by the Ministry of Labour and occupational diseases that are not listed but which can be proved to be the result of exposure to work. These include, injury benefit (80% of the gross wages lost for a maximum period of 78 weeks), various "social rehabilitation and supplementary benefits", including financial assistance to modify motor vehicles or homes, domestic help and psychosocial counselling and an injury pension, if earnings capacity has been reduced by at least 20% for a minimum of 26 weeks. The value of this injury pension varies with the degree of disability, but amounts to 66.7% of earnings at the maximum level. A distinctive feature of the pension benefit is that it is intended to partially compensate workers for "non-material" burdens. As a result it is paid regardless of whether or not a worker is in employment.

As regards rehabilitation, BGs pay for medical treatment (for an unlimited period) and provide a range of vocational rehabilitation services, including the provision of living expenses to workers and their families while rehabilitation is taking place. To support the rehabilitation process each BG employs full-time assistants to assess a worker's needs during initial medical treatment. It should additionally be noted that employers cannot dismiss severely disabled persons, that is those whose disability has been assessed at 50% or more, without obtaining permission from a public welfare authority.

The Netherlands

Under civil law an employer has to adapt work to an employee's capacities, a duty which in practice means that if a partially disabled employee makes an offer to do other work that is suitable the employer is in general required to accept that offer[29]. In addition, employers are required to submit a report on a work incapacitated employee to the social security agency within 13 weeks of the person reporting sick. This report has to be accompanied by a "work resumption plan" in which the employer reports on what has been done so far to promote job retention and what will be done in the future to facilitate work resumption. A failure to comply with these reporting requirements can lead to the postponement of the payment of disability benefit (see below) until 39 weeks after the actual report is submitted, during which time wages will have to be continued to be paid. A fine may also be imposed on employers if they fail to cooperate with the social security agency in taking action to facilitate work resumption.

More generally, it should be noted that employees who are work incapacitated may not be dismissed for two years. In addition, once this period has elapsed, the employer still cannot dismiss an employee without obtaining permission from the Employment Service. In considering whether to grant this permission the Employment Service will pay particular attention to the question of whether the employer has sufficiently proved that other (or adapted) work is unavailable.

Company doctors, who form part of the occupational health and safety services that all employers are required to have, play an important role in the design and implementation of work resumption plans. In many cases, however, their activities may be supported by rehabilitation services provided by insurers or outside specialist organisations.

Under the Sickness Benefit Act the employer is obliged to pay a non-temporary employee, who is sick for any reason, 70% of salary (or the national minimum wage, if this is greater) for the first year of sickness. After 52 weeks of sick leave an employee who is 33 years of age or older may be able to receive full or partial disability benefit under the Disability Benefits Act. The size of this benefit is determined by reference to the degree of an employee's disability. Thus, seven different categories of disability are distinguished and depending on which one an employee falls in, their benefit is set as a percentage of 100/108 times the daily wage. For example, an employee whose disability is assessed at between 15-25% receives 14% of this amount, while one whose disability is assessed at 80% or more obtains 70%.

The length of time during which employees initially receive disability benefit is determined by their age, with the length of entitlements ranging from half a year to six years. Once this period has elapsed employees may be entitled to a follow-up benefit which is payable until they reach retirement age. This benefit, which is also given to those under the age of 33, is calculated by adding to the national minimum wage two percent of the difference between the previous daily wage, up to a maximum in July 1997 of 297.51 Dfl (£93.56) for each year that a person is over 15 years of age. Once again the percentage of this figure that is paid is determined by the degree of a person's disability. Unemployed workers will in most cases also be entitled to unemployment or social assistance allowances.

Disablement benefits are funded solely by employer contributions. These contributions consist of two elements. First, a standard basic contribution which covers the costs of disability payments to the long-term disabled, that is those who have been disabled for more than five years. Secondly, a differentiated contribution which is set by reference to the size of the payments made to employees during the first five years of their disability. However, employers can apply to not make the latter contribution and bear the financial cost of the payments themselves, either directly or through insurance cover.

An important feature of the above benefit system is that its administration is assigned to a National Institute for Social Security whose executive board consists of representatives from employers' organisations, trade unions and members appointed by the Crown.

Sweden

Under the Work Environment Act 1977 employers are required to provide suitably organised activities for work adaption and rehabilitation[30]. The nature of these activities are spelt out in more detail via directives issued by the National Board of Occupational Safety and Health. These directives require, among other things, that:

- targets be set for work adaption and rehabilitation activities;
- regular checks be made on employees;
- work adaptions and rehabilitation required by employees commence as soon as possible;
- responsibilities in respect of work adaptions and rehabilitation be clarified and those undertaking such work have the necessary skills and competencies, as well as authority and resources;
- relevant activities be arranged in consultation with the individuals affected and their work environment representatives;
- annual reviews of the activities be conducted and any necessary changes made; and
- individual employee's work situations be adapted on the basis of his/her capacity for the task in question.

The above obligations are supplemented by further requirements under the General Insurance Act 1962 and the Act Concerning Certain Measures to Promote Employment of 1974. The first of these makes the employer of an insured person responsible, in consultation with the individual concerned, for ensuring that any rehabilitation needs are analysed as soon as possible and that any measures needed for effective rehabilitation are taken. It further provides for national insurance offices to coordinate and supervise the required rehabilitation activities. The second imposes a duty on employers to discuss with the County Labour Board measures to: improve the working conditions of elderly workers whose work capacity is reduced and safeguard their continued employment; and facilitate the recruitment of such employees and promote the employment of them.

No restrictions are imposed on employers as to how they source their rehabilitation services – which it should be noted don't extend to the provision of primary medical treatment. However, the largest provider of such services is Working Life Services, which is part of State's Labour Market Board.

As regards compensation, no distinction is drawn between work- and non-work related illness. Thus, during the first two weeks of sick leave, regardless of its cause, an employer is required to provide an employee with sick pay amounting to 80% of pay. After this two week period employees become entitled to sickness compensation paid by the social insurance office, which is paid at the same level. However, this compensation will be replaced by sickness benefit if it is considered that an employee's working capacity will be reduced for a year, but not permanently, and a work rehabilitation pro- gramme is not appropriate in the near future. Where an insured per- son's work capacity has been permanently reduced by at least a quarter, the individual concerned may be entitled to early retire- ment.

Sick pay, sickness compensation, sickness benefit and early retire- ment pensions can be divided by three-quarters, a half or a quarter, depending on the degree to which work capacity is reduced. Two other points concerning these arrangements also merit mentioning. First, each of the four forms of compensation can be paid to an indi- vidual with a job. Secondly, as a general rule, there is no question of employees being dismissed on the grounds of ill health while they are receiving sickness benefit.

United States of America (USA)

In the USA all states have workers' compensation laws that pro- vide benefits on a no-fault basis to workers in respect of work-relat- ed harm arising out of and in the course of employment. However, these state schemes differ considerably[31]. For example, in terms of the benefits provided, the provision made for vocational rehabilita- tion, the types of occupational ill health covered, and the criteria used to assess the work-relatedness of such ill health. In particular, a number of states do not compensate "psychological injuries" and limitations frequently apply with regard to the compensation of injuries caused by repetitive trauma, such as carpal tunnel syn- drome.

Most states, however, require the employer to provide full medical benefits, including medical rehabilitation. Cash benefits also typical- ly include: temporary total disability benefits, usually amounting to two-thirds of the pre-injury wage, subject to maximum and minimum amounts – the former ranging, in 1998, from $903 (£582.58) to $279.78 (£180.50); temporary partial disability benefits that generally provide a weekly payment equivalent to two-thirds of the difference between pre- and post-injury earnings; permanent partial disability benefits, although in most cases, only for a specified period of time; permanent total disability benefits, which again usually amount to two-thirds of the pre-injury wage, and are paid either for the duration of the disability or for life; and (weekly) death benefits, the level of which, in most states, is determined by the deceased's earnings and the number of survivors.

These benefits are funded by employer payroll taxes and provided (depending on the state) via one or more of the following mechanisms: insurance from a private insurance carrier; a state workers' compensation board or self-insurance. In the first two of these cases the premiums payable are determined by reference to the sector of industry in which the employer is engaged (manual rating) and, in the case of large employers, their claims experience (experience-rating).

It should be noted that workers' compensation benefits were explicitly designed as the exclusive remedy for work-related injuries and illness. However, in recent years this exclusivity doctrine has come under increasing legal challenge, particularly as a result of workers seeking common law damages for conditions which are not compensated under the workers' compensation system.

Not all state schemes lay down requirements in relation to vocational rehabilitation[32]. However, many do. Where this is the case, they may require a referral after a specified period of time, an evaluation by rehabilitation personnel in certain specified circumstances and the development of a rehabilitation services plan. It should, however, be noted that under the Americans with Disabilities Act employers are required to provide "reasonable accommodations" to disabled workers – such workers being defined in similar terms as under the DDA[33]. It also needs to be recognised that the need to control workers' compensation costs has prompted insurers, as well as many employers, to provide vocational rehabilitation services in order to assist workers to return to work more speedily.

The way forward

THE five sets of national arrangements relating to the compensation and rehabilitation of ill and injured workers exhibit marked differences. However, all provide workers with access to more generous benefits than are currently provided under the IIS in Britain. All also either impose far more onerous obligations on employers regarding the rehabilitation of ill and injured workers and/or provide greater incentives for them to engage in such activities.

In the area of compensation all the schemes reviewed provide compensation on a no-fault basis. However, significant differences exist with regard to the types of illnesses and injuries covered, the way in which compensation payments are funded, and the nature of the bodies that are responsible for their administration. For example, some schemes (Australia – New South Wales, Germany and the USA) apply only to work-related harm while others (Netherlands and Sweden) extend to cover illness and injury regardless of its source; in most of the countries, but not Sweden, compensation is funded exclusively by employers and to a greater or lesser extent the amount paid by individual employers is performance-rated; and in Germany, and the Netherlands, but not the other three, worker representatives are centrally involved in the management of the schemes at the industry and national levels respectively.

As regards vocational rehabilitation, three of the systems (Australia – New South Wales, the Netherlands and Sweden), place legal requirements on individual employers concerning the provision of such support to workers. Of the other two, one imposes obligations (extending to medical care) on sectoral insurance associations (Germany) while the fifth (the USA) incorporates medical treatment and sometimes (depending on the state) also lays down requirements in respect of vocational rehabilitation. In the case of Germany, the Netherlands and Sweden rehabilitation activity is, in turn, supported by statutory requirements relating to the use of occupational health services. Each of these countries also have mechanisms in place which serve to provide workers representatives with a substantial degree of control over the nature and operation of these activities and also either provide all ill and injured workers, or those who are severely disabled, with a substantial degree of job security.

In combination the various systems reviewed highlight a number of reforms that could be introduced to improve current British arrangements relating to the amelioration of work-related harm. However, it needs to be recognised that many of them face domestic political pressures because of the costs they impose on employers[34]. It also needs to be borne in mind that considerable care needs to be taken when considering the applicability of one country's arrangements to another. For they do not operate in isolation but are intimately connected with other social sub-systems, notably the surrounding systems of employment law, medical care and social security, as well as the broader political and cultural environment of the country concerned.

That said, in our view, the above review, when considered along-side the analysis provided in the earlier part of the chapter, suggests that serious consideration should be given to the following:

● the imposition of legal duties on employers to fund both "short-term" and "long-term" benefits to victims of work-related harm that are sufficient to cover a significant proportion of lost earnings;
● the establishment of mechanisms within this compensation system to encourage employers to prevent the occurrence of work-related harm;
● the placing of legal duties on employers regarding the provision and/or funding of rehabilitation for ill and injured workers; and
● the provision of much greater job security for ill and injured workers in order to facilitate the rehabilitation process.

Employer-funded compensation

The above review of the no-fault compensation arrangements which exist in five countries indicates that employer-funded compensation for work-related harm can be provided through a number of mechanisms: self-insurance, private insurance cover, sectoral insurance associations, and a national compensation fund. It further highlights the fact that these mechanisms do not have to be viewed as mutually exclusive and also draws attention to the fact that different arrangements can be used to provide "short-term" (ie. sickness) and "long-term" (ie. disability) benefits.

In short, a variety of different options exist with regard to the structuring of a new employer-funded system of compensation for work-related harm. The evaluation of these options is clearly a complex and far from easy task. It is, however, one that clearly needs to be carried out as a necessary first stage in the establishment of an equitable and just compensation system. We consequently urge the government to initiate such an evaluation, perhaps as part of a wider review of the legal framework relating to occupational health and safety (see chapter 6).

We further suggest that this evaluation extend to encompass two other important and related matters raised by the earlier national reviews. First, the question of whether there is a case for introducing a common compensation system for work- and non-work-related illness and injury as a means of avoiding the difficulties that surround the determination of the work-relatedness of many forms of ill health, including musculoskeletal disorders and stress. Secondly, the issue of what role should be played by personal injury litigation in the future.

In the meantime we put forward a number of proposals for discussion. These are:

- the introduction of a requirement on all employers to provide (either directly or through insurance cover) full sick pay for a period of a year to those who execute work or labour for them, unless this work is carried out as part of the activities of an economically independent business;

- the establishment of a system of employer-funded sectoral insurance associations to administer the provision of longer-term (pre-retirement) benefits which are sufficient to cover a significant proportion of the earnings lost by workers as a result of illness and injury (see below). This system might be restricted to work-related harm, defined to encompass all conditions currently covered by the IIS and the European List of occupational diseases. Alternatively, it might extend to cover all forms of illness and injury, regardless of their cause;

- the creation of a "fall-back" state compensation system which provides equivalent benefits to those workers, who for one reason or another, are excluded from the coverage of these benefit arrangements; and

- the retention of personal injury litigation as an option for workers who either cannot obtain compensation under the above arrangements or feel that it offers them a means of obtaining higher levels of compensation. Any compensation provided through such litigation should continue to be funded by a compulsory system of employers' liability insurance – albeit one that has been amended to address the weaknesses identified earlier in the current statutory framework[35]. However, courts should be empowered to award punitive damages and to consider breach of statutory duty claims under the general duties of the HSW Act and the MHSW Regulations.

Employer supported rehabilitation

Rehabilitation, by definition, has to be geared to the needs of the individual concerned. Consequently, the identification of what rehabilitation is required is arguably best done at the workplace level where detailed knowledge exists on such issues as current work tasks, possible alternative jobs and the types of work adaptions that can be made. Two ways of achieving this workplace focus can be identified. One is to place duties on employers with regard to such matters as the appointment of rehabilitation coordinators and the development of rehabilitation plans – issues which we have seen are addressed in three of the national schemes reviewed: Australia –

New South Wales, the Netherlands and Sweden. The other is to follow the German approach and entrust these tasks to officials from the body (or bodies) which provide no-fault compensation to ill and injured workers.

Both of these approaches have potential strengths and weaknesses. However, if, as suggested above, employers were required to provide sick pay for a year, then the former would seem to be preferable.

In many cases ill and injured workers will require medical treatment. An important role of "rehabilitation coordinators" will therefore be to liaise with relevant medical practitioners. However, given the inadequacies in the vocational rehabilitation services offered by the NHS and other government services identified earlier, there is a clear case for employers to also be required to themselves provide or fund such rehabilitation. Once again two broad ways of doing this can be identified which parallel those described above in respect of the determination of rehabilitation needs. These are via employer use of multi-disciplinary occupational health and safety services, supplemented where necessary by outside providers, or through rehabilitation services provided by the organisation(s) responsible for administering the compensation system. As with the initial evaluation of rehabilitation needs, however, the former approach would seem the more appropriate in a system under which employers are responsible for the payment of short-term sick pay.

Whichever of these approaches, however, is considered more appropriate there is a clear need for workers to have some say over the services they receive and some protection against attempts to pressure them back to work before they are ready. Consequently, it is important that their operation is controlled jointly by employer and worker representatives.

Employer provided rehabilitation could be funded directly by large employers. The costs involved, however, would be likely to be too great for many smaller employers. As a result some mechanism would need to be put in place to subsidise their costs. One way of doing this would be to establish regional occupational health and safety services, perhaps within the NHS. Another would be to utilise the no-fault compensation system to support the establishment of multi-disciplinary occupational health and safety services containing the necessary expertise. Once again, however, these services should be controlled jointly in order to ensure that they operate in an appropriate and supportive manner.

Indeed the role played by the industry-based insurance associations in German serves to raise a further issue of considerable importance, namely whether there is a case for incorporating the provision of medical treatment into any future no-fault compensation system. Unfortunately, we remain unclear as to the desirability or otherwise of this, not least because the question raises a host of fundamental issues concerning the future role of the NHS, including that of GPs. It does, however, appear to merit serious discussion, particularly if a work-related compensation scheme was preferred, given the observations made earlier about the current inadequacies in NHS provision and the degree to which the service currently subsidises employers.

We are, however, clear on two further related matters. First, that the employer's duty to fund non-medical rehabilitation should apply to all ill and injured workers because of the problems associated with identifying work-relatedness mentioned earlier. Secondly, that the current provision made for the treatment of occupational ill health within the NHS needs to be urgently reviewed and improved. For even if arrangements were established under which much of the responsibility for organising its treatment were moved elsewhere, there would still be a substantial role for the NHS in respect of the self-employed and other categories of workers who, for one reason or another, fell outside the scope of the new arrangements. It therefore seems desirable that Directors of Public Health be required in future to evaluate the scale of work-related ill health falling within health authority or primary care group areas in order to (a) advise those who commission primary and secondary care of the specialist treatment services that need to be put in place; and (b) identify the additional specialist skills that are required to meet those needs.

Encouraging prevention

A move to a no-fault compensation system which not only provides much improved benefits but requires employers to fund them would seem likely to encourage employers to examine ways of keeping their costs down. Certainly there is some evidence from North America to suggest that the cost of workers' compensation premiums have led employers to take action to prevent accidents at work[36].

However, as we have seen, the no-fault compensation systems in Australia – New South Wales, Germany, the Netherlands and the USA all attempt to further encourage employers to reduce worker injury and illness by experience-rating their contributions. How far such rating does in fact encourage employers to take action to reduce worker illness or injury, however, remains uncertain. A number of North American studies have, for example, investigated whether its use appears to be associated with better accident rates. Some of these have found evidence to suggest that it is, while others have not. The balance of evidence, however, tends to support the former position[37].

Given this, there would seem grounds for making use of experience-rating. However, the conflicting nature of the USA evidence, as well as the difficulties of applying such a rating process to small employers, suggests that there is a case for more directly encouraging the prevention of work-related harm by linking employer contributions to an evaluation of the standards of their preventive organisation and arrangements[38]. One option in this area would be to impose an obligation on the proposed sectoral insurance associations to conduct periodic inspections of all workplaces and to utilise their results when setting premiums. Another would be for them to offer a service whereby employers could submit themselves to an audit and thereby potentially make themselves eligible for a premium discount.

More generally, it should be noted that sectoral insurance associations could make an important contribution to the implementation of a number of the recommendations put forward in previous chapters. First, by providing an infrastructure to support the greater use of industry-based regulations and ACOPs. Secondly, if placed under the joint control of employers and trade unions, by substantially strengthening the joint regulation of workplace health and safety at the industry level. Thirdly, by funding industry-based systems of roving safety representatives and, as already noted, regional occupational health and safety services which could be utilised by SMEs. Fourthly, by providing employers with an additional source of health and safety advice and in doing so supporting a shift towards a more rigorous approach to enforcement on the part of HSE and local authority inspectors. The potential value of using such insurance associations to support greater sectoral regulation of health and safety issues is moreover highlighted by a recent Dutch government initiative to encourage industry level agreements on such matters as stress, overuse injuries, allergies, noise, lifting, solvent brain damage and silicosis[39].

Conclusion

THIS chapter initially provided a review of the current provision made by employers in respect of the compensation and rehabilitation of workers injured and made ill by their work activities. This review revealed that the provision made in both of these areas is often very limited and in doing so drew attention to the fact that it is the workers most likely to be harmed by their work who are frequently among those in the least favourable position. It further highlighted the fact that the current weaknesses in employer activities in these two areas is compounded by weaknesses in existing, and related, state arrangements.

A number of proposals that have been put forward to improve this situation, such as introducing experience-rating into the IIS and employers' liability insurance, the reclaiming of the costs incurred by the NHS in treating the victims of work-related harm, and the introduction of a requirement on employers' liability insurers to take action to rehabilitate ill and injured workers, were then outlined and discussed. It was concluded that while all of them have attractions, they also have important limitations. As a result it was further concluded that more radical action was needed.

Following a review of the arrangements utilised to compensate and rehabilitate ill and injured workers in five other countries, the chapter went on to argue that serious consideration be given to the following:

- the imposition of legal duties on employers to fund both "short-term" and "long-term" benefits to victims of work-related harm that are sufficient to cover a significant proportion of lost earnings;
- the establishment of mechanisms within this compensation system to encourage employers to prevent the occurrence of work-related harm;
- the placing of legal duties on employers regarding the provision and/or funding of rehabilitation for ill and injured workers; and
- the provision of much greater job security for ill and injured workers in order to facilitate the rehabilitation process.

Possible ways of achieving these objectives were subsequently discussed. In particular, it was suggested that employers be required to provide full sick pay for a year; that a system of sectoral insurance associations be established to provide longer-term benefits, either in respect of work-related injuries and ill health or all forms of worker injury and illness; that the role of these associations extend to their involvement in the development of industry-based regulations and ACOPs, and the establishment of regional occupational health and safety services for use by SMEs; and that employers be required to appoint rehabilitation coordinators and to use such services to provide workers with access to appropriate vocational rehabilitation, regardless of the source of their injury and illness.

More generally, the chapter called for urgent action to be taken to improve the NHS's current provision for the treatment of occupational injuries and ill health, and proposed that the government undertake a major evaluation of the viability of the above proposals and other alternative means of achieving the objectives that underlay them.

Summary of key points

Amelioration of work-related harm

- introduction of a requirement on all employers to provide full sick pay for a period of a year to those who execute work or labour for them, unless this work is carried out as part of the activities of an economically independent business;
- establishment of a system of employer-funded sectoral insurance associations to administer the provision of longer-term, earnings-related, benefits to either those suffering from work-related harm or those suffering from any form of illness and injury;
- creation of a system under which employer contributions to these associations vary according to their claims experience and/or standards of health and safety prevention;
- use of the above associations to provide health and safety advice to employers, fund regional occupational health and safety services and industry-based systems of roving safety representatives, and support the development of industry-based regulations and ACOPs;
- retention of personal injury litigation as an option for workers who either cannot obtain compensation under the above arrangements or feel it offers them a means of obtaining higher levels of compensation;
- empowerment of the courts to hear breach of statutory duty claims in respect of the general duties of the HSW Act and the Management of Health and Safety at Work Regulations, and to award punitive damages in cases where an employer has recklessly exposed workers to risk
- imposition on employers of duties concerning the appointment of rehabilitation coordinators and the development of rehabilitation plans in respect of all ill and injured workers whose absence exceeds, or is likely to exceed, a specified length of time;
- introduction of duties on employers to provide vocational rehabilitation through occupational health and safety services;
- action to improve the current provision made for the treatment of occupational ill health within the NHS; and
- investigation into the future role of the NHS in treating ill and injured workers.

Notes

1 *Revitalising Health and Safety*, HSC/DETR Consultation Document, July 1999.

2 *Revitalising Health and Safety*, op cit; and J.R. Jones, J.T. Hodgson, T.A. Clegg and R.C. Elliott, *Self-reported Work-related Illness*, 1998, HSE Books.

3 N. Davies and P. Teasdale, *The Costs to the British Economy of Work Accidents and Work-Related Ill Health*, 1990, HSE Books.

4 Confederation of British Industry, *Managing Absence: 1995* CBI/Centre-File Survey Results, 1995, Confederation of British Industry.

5 Law Commission, *Personal Injury Compensation: How Much is Enough?*, Report No.225, 1994, HMSO.

6 D. Collinson, *"Shifting Lives: Work-Home Pressures in the North Sea Oil Industry"*, CRSA/RCSA, 35(3), 1998, 301-324.

7 O. Rowlands, N. Singleton, J. Maher and V. Higgins, *Living in Britain: Results from the 1995 General Household Survey*, 1997, Stationary Office.

8 N. Terry and P. White, "Occupational Pension Schemes and their interaction with HRM", *Human Resource Management Journal*, 8(4), 1998, 20-36.

9 *The Financial Marketing Pocket Book 1998*, 1998, NTC Publications.

10 See Employers' Liability (Compulsory Insurance) Act 1969.

11 See C. Parsons, "Employers' Liability Insurance – How Secure is the System?", *Industrial Law Journal*, 28(2), 1999, 109-132.

12 For a more detailed critique of the statutory framework see Parsons, 1990, op cit.

13 Reference in current endnote 11; and *Report of the Royal Commission on Civil Liability and Compensation for Personal Injury*, Cmnd 7054, 1978, HMSO.

14 K. Bunt, *Occupational Health Provision at Work*, Contract Research Report 57/1993, Health and Safety Executive.

15 B. Erens and D. Ghate, *Invalidity Benefit: A Longitudinal Survey of New Recipients*, Department of Social Security, Research Report No.20, 1993, HMSO.

16 I. Cunningham and P. James, "Absence and Return to Work: Towards a Research Agenda", *Personnel Review*, forthcoming; and N. Meager, P. Bates, S. Dench and M. Williams, *Employment of Disabled People: Assessing the Extent of Participation*, 1998, DfEE Publications.

17 Jones et al, op cit.

18 Ibid.

19 "Unification Theory: The Birth of Integrated Healthcare", *Employee Health Bulletin*, 4, 1998, 10-14.

20 For a useful overview of the current position in these areas see S. Duckworth, P. McGeer, D. Kearns and P. Thornton, International Research Project on *Job Retention and Return to Work Strategies for Disabled Workers: Study Report – United Kingdom*, 1998, International Labour Organisation.

21 Also see *Treatment for People with Work Related Upper Limb Disorders*, 1994, Trades Union Congress; and *Enquiry into the Training of Healthcare Professionals who come into contact with Skin Diseases*, 1998, All Parliamentary Group on Skin.

22 Duckworth et al, 1998, op cit.

23 H. Morrison, "Rehabilitation and Return to Work: Do Other Countries Succeed?", *Work*, 3, 48-54.

---

24 S. Sugarman, "Personal Injury Law Reform: A Proposed First Step", *Industrial Law Journal*, 16(3), 1987, 30-45. More generally see Report of the Royal Commission on *Civil Liability and Compensation for Personal Injury*, Cmnd 7054, 1978, HMSO.

25 The UK Employers' Liability Insurance Market, Information Sheet L620, Association of British Insurers.

26 The summary that follows draws heavily on H. Biggs, International Research Project on *Job Retention/Return to Work Strategies for Disabled Workers: Australia – Interim Report*, 1998, International Labour Organisation.

27 Also see D. Kenny, "Occupational Rehabilitation Assessed: The Verdict of Employers", *Journal of Occupational Health and Safety*, 12(2), 145-153.

28 The material provided in this section is drawn from the following reports: A. Martin, A. Linehan and I. Whitehouse, *The Regulation of Health and Safety in Five European Countries: Denmark, France, Germany, Spain and Italy with a Supplement on Recent Developments in the Netherlands*, HSE Contract Research Report No.84/1996, 1996, HSE Books; and M. Albrecht and H. Braun, International Research Project on *Job Retention and Return to Work Strategies for Disabled Workers: Study Report - Germany*, 1998, International Labour Organisation.

29 This section is based on material drawn from the following report: B. Cuelenaere and R. Prins, International Research Project on *Job Retention and Return to Work Strategies for Disabled Workers: Study Report – Netherlands*, 1998, International Labour Organisation.

30 This summary is based on the following report: A. Karlsson, International Research Project on *Job Retention and Return to Work Strategies for Disabled Workers: Study Report – Sweden*, 1998, International Labour Organisation.

31 Except where noted, this section is drawn from E. Spieler and J. Burton, "Compensation for Disabled Workers: Workers' Compensation" in T. Thomason, J. Burton, and D. Hyatt (ed), *New Approaches to Disability Management in the Workplace*, 1998, Industrial Relations Research Association.

32 See M. Berkowitz and D. Dean, *"Facilitating Employment through Vocational Rehabilitation"* in T. Thomason et al, 1998, op cit.

33 See S. Bruyere and P. James, "Disability Management and the Disability Discrimination Act", *Human Resource Management Journal*, 7(2), 1997, 3-15.

34 See L. Aarts, R. Burkhauser, and P. de Jong, *"Convergence: A Comparison of European and United States Disability Policies"* in T. Thomason et al, 1998, op cit.

35 However, since the proposed compensation arrangements would be likely to reduce substantially the use made of personal linjury litigation, the cost of such insurance, which can sometimes amount to 10% of payroll, would presumably also drop considerably. See Sugarman, 1987, op cit.

36 D. Durbin and R. Butler, *"Prevention of Disability from Work-related Sources: The Roles of Risk Management, Government Intervention and Insurance"* in T. Thomason et al, 1998, op cit.

37 Ibid. Also see J. Burton and J. Chelius, "Workplace Safety and Health Regulations: Rationale and Results" in B. Kaufman (ed), *Government Regulation of the Employment Relationship*, 1997, Industrial Relations Research Association.

38 See *Economic Incentives to Improve the Working Environment: Summary and*

Conclusions of an International Study, 1994, European Foundation for the Improvement of Living and Working Conditions.

39 "Government to help Employers and Unions 'go Dutch'", *Health and Safety Bulletin,* 280, July/August 1998, 4.

Conclusion

The way forward

THIS book has been concerned with providing a critical evaluation of the present legal framework for occupational health and
safety. Its conclusions point to the fact that, notwithstanding the
improvements in both the content and administration of the law
introduced by the Health and Safety at Work (HSW) Act 1974, the
present scale of work-related harm remains massive. For example,
over a million workers each year suffer an accident at work, more
than two million people suffer from an illness which they believe has
been caused or made worse by their work, and in excess of 25,000
workers permanently leave the labour force each year as a result of
work-related injuries and illnesses. It further indicates that many
employers, particularly small and medium-sized enterprises (SMEs),
have neither the capability or willingness to put in place the arrangements that are seen as central to the effective management of health
and safety.

The scale of this harm and the failure of employers to take adequate action to protect workers from work-related injuries and ill
health casts grave doubt on the validity of the self-regulatory philosophy advocated by the Robens Committee and subsequently incorporated into the HSW Act. It also points to the fact that the current
legal framework needs to be significantly improved.

Most, if not all, of the weaknesses identified in the legal framework were present from the outset. For example, the lack of statutory requirements on the appointment of occupational health and
safety specialists, insufficient guidance on how health and safety
should be managed, inadequate arrangements to compensate the
victims of work-related harm and provide them with rehabilitative
support and the adoption of an enforcement policy which placed too
great a reliance on the provision of advice and persuasion. However,
their significance has been accentuated by economic and social
changes that have occurred since the introduction of the HSW Act.
These changes have included a growth of employment in SMEs, the
introduction of more devolved systems of management in larger

organisations, a reduction in trade union membership and recognition, shifts in the composition of employment away from manufacturing industry, a rise in the use of 'non-standard forms of employment', cuts in social welfare and inspectorate resources, and the introduction of more intensive work patterns.

Not all of these changes have had adverse consequences. Thus, the shift of employment away from such sectors as mining and manufacturing, have resulted in a reduction in fatal accidents. Overall, however, they have not only created an environment very different to that which prevailed at the time of the Robens Committee, but one that is far less conducive to a legal framework that is premised on encouraging voluntary, self-regulatory behaviour on the part of employers and workers and their representatives.

Rationale for reform

IN the preceding chapters we have identified a range of reforms to address the above problems and challenges. These reforms, which are summarised below, are intended, in combination, to achieve the following four objectives:

- to lay down clearer and more onerous statutory duties on employers, particularly with regard to the management 'organisation and arrangements' that need to be put in place;
- to ensure that employers have access to necessary specialist expertise through the imposition of requirements concerning the use of multi-disciplinary occupational health and safety services;
- to encourage and enable employers to adopt a broader and more holistic approach to the issue of 'health and safety at work' which accords adequate recognition to the fact that much of the work-related harm experienced by workers stems not just from accidents or 'traditional' occupational diseases, but consists of musculoskeletal disorders and stress-related illnesses. That is an approach which gives adequate recognition to the fact that the protection of workers encompasses not only preventing exposure to dangerous machinery and hazardous substances, but the creation of working environments that take adequate account of their physical and mental capabilities;
- to encourage employers to accord health and safety at work a higher priority by (a) increasing the likelihood of non-compliance being identified and meaningfully penalised; (b) extending the coverage and effectiveness of systems of worker representation; and (c) creating a compensation system that provides employers with a financial incentive to reduce work-related harm.

It is recognised that the reforms put forward to achieve these objectives will impose additional costs on both employers and government. In our view these costs can be defended on the grounds that the current scale of pain, suffering and financial loss inflicted on workers through work-related injuries and ill health is morally and socially unacceptable. However, we further believe that the proposed reforms can be defended on two other grounds. First, they would contribute to the creation of a legal framework that is more in line with the requirements and philosophy of European legislation on health and safety. Secondly, they embody a recognition that the prevention of work-related harm and the amelioration of its consequences for workers, employers and the taxpayer should be seen as being inter-related rather than distinct areas of concern.

The HSE has estimated that in 1990 work-related accidents and ill health cost British employers between £4.5 billion and £9.5 billion – figures that represented between 5% and 10% of all UK industrial companies' gross trading profits during that year. It further estimated that, when social security and National Health Service costs were added, these figures rose to between £11 billion and £16 billion, or 1-2% of Gross Domestic Product. These costs are clearly enormous. A large proportion of them are also unnecessary and avoidable. Given this, the costs associated with the reforms proposed clearly need to be considered alongside the potentially considerable savings that they could offer through reducing the scale of work-related harm.

The present government, to its credit, has already gone someway to acknowledging this last point, notably through discussions that have taken place concerning the possible reform of the Industrial Injuries Scheme (IIS) to establish closer linkages between compensation, prevention and rehabilitation and its more general advocacy of 'joined-up government'. However, the analysis presented points to the fact that the creation of a greater degree of integration between these three areas of activity is not just an issue relevant to the structure of the IIS, but is one that needs to be pursued on a much more wide-ranging basis and hence encompass a consideration of a host of other relevant, and inter-related, issues. For example, the relative importance to be attached to personal injury litigation and no-fault sources of compensation; the role of the National Health Service in the treatment of work-related harm and how this role is to be funded; and the obligations to be imposed on employers in respect of both the rehabilitation of workers and the provision and financing of compensation to those injured and made ill by their work.

The reform proposals: summary of key points

THE key reforms we have proposed are summarised below under the chapter headings to which they relate – employers and their legal duties; the administration of the statutory framework; worker representation; and the amelioration of work-related harm.

Employers and their legal duties

- amendment of the general duties laid down under sections 2 and 3 of the HSW Act so that they specify in broad terms the management "organisation and arrangements" that employers need to put in place in respect of the management of health and safety at work, as well as the preventive principles that should inform their development;
- removal of the qualification of the above duties in terms of reasonable practicability and its replacement by one that requires employer actions to be evaluated in terms of their adequacy;
- the introduction of an Approved Code of Practice (ACOP) to provide detailed guidance on these revised duties;
- making of new regulations on the management of road transport risks, temporary working and sub-contracting, and the ergonomic design of work tasks and schedules;
- creation of a statutory framework under which all employers would be required to have access, either internally or through accredited external providers, to occupational health and safety services of a specified quality;
- the placing of these services under the joint control of employer and worker representatives;
- reduction in the reliance placed on goal-orientated regulatory duties; and
- the increased use of sectoral-specific regulations and ACOPs.

Administration of the statutory framework

- investigation into the effectiveness of the tripartite structure of the Health and Safety Commission (HSC) in order to evaluate whether there is a case for expanding its membership to encompass a wider range of interest groups;
- establishment of a system of HSC regional consultative committees along the lines of the Environmental Protection Advisory Councils set up by the Environment Agency;
- investigation into desirability (and scale) of local authority involvement in the enforcement of health and safety law

---

- action to achieve greater consistency between local authorities in terms of enforcement action and Environmental Health Officer staffing levels;
- adoption of a more rigorous enforcement policy on the part of HSE and local authority inspectors, and within this the placing of more emphasis on the use of prosecutions combined with a greater willingness to take cases on indictment;
- supplementation of HSE and local authority inspections by the introduction of statutory requirements on the carrying out of "third party" audits on employer health and safety arrangements and performance;
- imposition of an explicit health and safety duty on company directors;
- removal of current restrictions on the use of imprisonment as a penalty for breaches of health and safety law;
- possible introduction of "proportionate" and "equity" fines for health and safety offences and the use of pre-sentencing reports;
- provision of court powers to make probation orders requiring organisations to take specified steps to improve their health and safety arrangements;
- strengthening of the current protocol on the investigation of workplace deaths along with the introduction of the Law Commission's proposed offence of "corporate killing";
- enhanced right for workers and their trade unions to initiate private prosecutions in respect of breaches of health and safety laws;
- considerable expansion of HSE resources to support a substantial increase in inspectors, support the adoption of a more rigorous enforcement policy and an expansion in internal and commissioned research.

Worker representation

- increased rights to safety representatives and trade unions to enforce statutory provisions on worker representation;
- introduction of measures to allow trade unions to represent members, whether or not they work for an employer who recognises them for the purposes of collective bargaining;
- action to establish systems of mobile safety representatives covering small firms;
- provision to safety representative of powers to issue 'provisional improvement notices' where they believe there to be a serious infringement of health and safety standards and to 'stop the job' where they believe there is a serious and imminent risk to workers;

- introduction of legal rights to safety representatives regarding the establishment, role and operation of occupational health and safety services;
- imposition of more onerous obligations on employers to provide safety representatives with 'health and safety' time to undergo training and carry out their statutory functions;
- introduction of a right for safety representatives to require information from suppliers of articles and substances;
- adoption by HSE and local authority inspectors of a more rigorous approach to the enforcement of representational rights and within this, the according of greater recognition to the need for safety representatives to adopt a more "holistic" role in respect of the protection of worker health and safety; and
- establishment of a general legal framework for worker representation (along the lines of the works council systems used within other European countries) to act as a "fall back" position in situations where trade unions are not recognised to ensure that health and safety representation is located and supported by broader mechanisms of worker representation.

Amelioration of work-related harm

- introduction of a requirement on all employers to provide full sick pay for a period of a year to those who execute work or labour for them, unless this work is carried out as part of the activities of an economically independent business;
- establishment of a system of employer-funded sectoral insurance associations to administer the provision of longer-term, earnings-related, benefits to either those suffering from work-related harm or those suffering from any form of illness and injury;
- creation of a system under which employer contributions to these associations vary according to their claims experience and/or standards of health and safety prevention;
- use of the above associations to provide health and safety advice to employers, fund regional occupational health and safety services and industry-based systems of roving safety representatives, and support the development of industry-based regulations and ACOPs;
- retention of personal injury litigation as an option for workers who either cannot obtain compensation under the above arrangements or feel it offers them a means of obtaining higher levels of compensation;
- empowerment of the courts to hear breach of statutory duty claims in respect of the general duties of the HSW Act and the Management of Health and Safety at Work Regulations, and to

award punitive damages in cases where an employer has recklessly exposed workers to risk

- imposition on employers of duties concerning the appointment of rehabilitation coordinators and the development of rehabilitation plans in respect of all ill and injured workers whose absence exceeds, or is likely to exceed, a specified length of time;
- introduction of duties on employers to provide vocational rehabilitation through occupational health and safety services;
- action to improve the current provision made for the treatment of occupational ill health within the NHS; and
- investigation into the future role of the NHS in treating ill and injured workers.

Some of the above reforms could be introduced through regulations and ACOPs made under the HSW Act. Others, notably those concerning employer health and safety "organisation and arrangements" and penalties for breaches of statutory duties, could be implemented by amending, albeit significantly, the Act itself. A number of other proposals, however, such as those relating to the establishment and role of sectoral-insurance associations and employer obligations in respect of the rehabilitation of ill and injured workers, could less easily be accommodated through either of these avenues.

Given this, there seem two options available as regards the implementation of the proposals put forward in these areas. The first is to introduce them by means of a separate statute. The second is to replace the HSW Act by a broader-based statute which addresses not only the prevention of work-related harm, but the provision of compensation and rehabilitation to the victims of such harm. On balance, we feel the second of these options is to be preferred for three main reasons. First, it would be tidier and hence more clearly create an awareness on the part of employers that the management of health and safety, and the costs and benefits associated with it, need to be viewed in a much wider context than is currently the case. Secondly, it would consequently be more likely to stimulate the adoption of a more integrated approach to health and safety management which embodies a much greater degree of coordination between safety specialists, occupational health practitioners and human resource staff. Finally, it would facilitiate a role for the HSE in monitoring the operation of the sectoral-insurance associations and employer compliance with their obligations relating to the rehabilitation of workers.

Conclusion : **The way forward**

Appendix one

Committees of enquiry

A S part of the consultation process for this project, each of our Specialist Groups held a committee of enquiry to which they invited expert witnesses to give written or oral evidence before a panel of experts. The expert witnesses were provided with a series of questions which were intended to act as a guide to the areas of enquiry to be pursued during the hearings. The expert witnesses were also invited to supplement the questions if they felt we had overlooked an issue of importance.

Below is a list of the hearings, the panels of experts, the expert witnesses and the questions as circulated.

1. The Management of Health and Safety

Panel of experts: Mathias Beck; Professor Phil James; Professor Steven Tombs; Dr Charles Woolfson

Expert witnesses: John Barrell (IOSH); Nigel Bryson (GMB); Richard Clifton (HSE); Dr Anna Rowbotham (RoSPA); Roger Spiller (MSF)

Written evidence was submitted by the Federation of Small Businesses

Supporting MP: John Cryer

Questions

1. How far do employers adequately prioritise the issue of health and safety?
2. How adequate are current organisational arrangements relating to the management of health and safety at work?
3. What improvements are needed in the following areas:
   a. health and safety policies and planning?
   b. carrying out risk assessments and the implementation of the findings of such assessments?
   c. provision of information and training?
   d. the role of line managers?
   e. worker representation and involvement?
   f. use of occupational health and safety specialists and services?

g. adoption of auditing and other specialist health and safety systems, including those contained in British and international standards?
h. management of sub-contractors and workers engaged on such 'non-standard' forms of employment, such as temporary workers and homeworkers?
i. monitoring and measurement of standards of health and safety management and performance?
j. the relationship that exists between health and safety management and other aspects of organisational operation?
4. What legal changes are needed to encourage these improvements?
5. How can the HSE and Local Authorities better encourage improved standards of health and safety management?
6. What actions are needed to support and improve health and safety standards in small and medium sized enterprises?
7. How far is action needed to improve current arrangements relating to the education and training of health and safety specialists?
8. To what extent is action needed to strengthen health and safety activity at the regional and sectoral levels?
9. Is action needed to encourage the use and/or certification of commercial safety management schemes?
10. Is there a need to extend the use of licensing to a greater range of activities and to those carrying out particular types of health and safety activities?

2. Administrative Authorities

Panel of experts: David Bergman; Phil Carpenter; Roslyn Perkins
Expert witnesses: Richard Clifton (HSE); Brian Etheridge (Local Authority Unit); Bud Hudspith (GPMU); David Morris (HSE)
Supporting MP: Jim Fitzpatrick
Questions
1. How effective is the current relationship between the Health and Safety Commission and the Health and Safety Executive?
2. Is the 'tripartite' structure of the Commission still relevant to current employment and social conditions?
3. Is the division of work/responsibility between the Health and Safety Executive and Local Authorities appropriate?
4. How effective is HSE's/Local Authorities' work in relation to:
    a. preventative inspection
    b. investigation of injury, death and disease
    c. prosecution policy
    and how could it be improved?
5. Does the HSE/Local Authority deal appropriately with:
    a. hazards faced by homeworkers?
    b. 'new' hazards like stress?
    c. hazards from new forms of technology?
6. What reforms could be made to increase the effectiveness of EMAS?
7. Should there be changes made to the structure of offences contained in the HASWA 1974?
8. Should health and safety duties be imposed upon directors?

9. In general terms do sufficient sanctions exist to:
   a. deter companies from breaking health and safety law, and
   b. punish those companies which do break the law?
10. Standard setting: how can the drafting of regulations and ACOPs be improved to provide SMEs with a clearer understanding of their legal duties?
11. How adequate are the arrangements in place for standard setting in respect of hazardous substances?
12. Does the present system of IACs provide an adequate basis for the discussion of health and safety issues at the sectoral level?
13. Should insurance companies have an additional role in maintaining and enforcing health and safety standards?

3. Trade Union and Worker Representation

Panel of experts: Nigel Bryson (GMB); Professor Phil James; Andrea Oates; Graham Petersen; Dr David Walters

Expert witnesses: George Brumwell (UCATT); Richard Clifton (HSE); Guy Dean (Public Concern at Work); Mike Holder (Hazards); Sophy Mangera (Health Works in Newham); Doug Russell (USDAW)

Supporting MPs: John Cryer and Eileen Gordon

Questions

1. Are you satisfied with the current arrangements for worker involvement in occupational health and safety?
2. Do the current legislative arrangements allow a satisfactory input for the kind of people that you represent?
3. What additional rights or changes would you like to see in the present arrangements in relation to:
   a. enforcement, for example concerning:
      i. the role of inspectors?
      ii. the role of employment tribunals and the courts?
      iii. the use of private prosecutions?
   b. provisional improvement notices?
   c. stopping the job?
   d. access to HSE inspectors?
   e. the role of safety representatives in relation to:
      i. planning health and safety arrangements?
      ii. deciding on the use of occupational health and safety services?
      iii. risk assessment?
   f. widening of the health and safety function to include representation on environmental issues?
   g. any other arrangements?
4. Are current arrangements adequate for the representation of workers in small enterprises?
5. What forms of additional support are required, for example, in relation to:
   a. the employer's obligations to facilitate the election of health and safety representatives?
   b. time-off for health and safety representatives to carry out their functions and to receive training?

---

c. improving recognition of the competencies of health and safety representatives?

d. dealing with questions of recognition and the operation of health and safety representatives in such situations as small workplaces or multi-employer worksites, workplaces where there is no union recognition and workplaces where there is recognition but no safety rep?

e. health and safety representatives' rights to receive information?

f. to prevent victimisation of health and safety representatives?

6. How could changes and additional support for the existing system of worker representation in health and safety be best resourced? Is there a role for a Work Environment Fund and if so, what form should it take?

7. Should Approved Codes of Practice be used to develop details of arrangements which cannot be easily included in Regulations but which nevertheless require some legal authority? For example:

a. set standards of competence for health and safety representatives

b. provide more support for trade union training through setting training quality standards that are linked to competence

c. provide systems for accreditation and certification of training provision

d. oblige inspectors of regulatory agencies to consult with health and safety representatives

e. provide structured and detailed requirements concerning employers' obligations to facilitate the election of health and safety representatives and the creation of joint safety committees

f. provide structured and detailed requirements on the obligations of employers to ensure the facilitation of representation and consultation with representatives when undertaking their obligations on health and safety management defined in other regulations

g. provide means for health and safety representatives, as representatives of users, to require information from suppliers on the safe and healthy use of articles and substances

h. improve the practical operation of measures to protect health and safety representatives from victimisation by employers

8. Is there a need for a wider framework of legislation in which representational rights on health and safety would be part of wider rights to representation?

9. In addition to rights on representation, is there a need to enhance individual rights to participation on health and safety? For example, to provide more specific rights to refuse dangerous work or for individuals to be entitled to information on hazards associated with work?

10. Should representation be based on 'workers' rather than 'employees' to take account of changes in employment?

4. Nature and Scale of Work Related Harm

Panel of experts: Professor Phil James; Carolyn Jones; Simon Pickvance

Expert witnesses: Patricia Thornton (University of York); Wendy Lawrence (RSI Association); Colin Ettinger (Irwin Mitchel Solicitors); Howard Saunders (HSE); Professor Nick Wikeley (University of Southampton)

Supporting MP: Jim Fitzpatrick

Questions

1. Services for sufferers from work related ill-health
   a. What kind of services should be available in the workplace and within the NHS for sufferers from work-related ill-health?
   b. What should the role of primary care be: central, one component, safety net only?
   c. Should employers' prevention services double as personnel services (eg. sickness absence monitoring)?
   d. Are current codes of practice and regulations on confidentiality and access to records and reports adequate, eg. in small firms?
   e. How should services be funded? (employers, tax, EL insurance, hypothecated fund, NHS)
   f. How can the lack of specialist skills in the acute sector be addressed?
2. Civil compensation
   a. How can inequities of access to the law be tackled?
   b. Should the limitation period be altered?
   c. What can we do about the dearth of suitable expert witnesses (particularly in the light of 'fast-track and small-claims track compensation')?
   d. What are the advantages/disadvantages of no-fault compensation rather than litigation?
   e. What should be done about inadequate levels of compensation, privacy clauses, restrictions of employers' liability?
3. Social security
   a. Has the Industrial Injuries Scheme got a future?
   b. Can the occupational preference be justified?
   c. Should we replace it by a system of comprehensive disability benefit?
   d. How can inequities of access to IIS be addressed (ie. women, non-manual trades, etc)?
   e. How can administration of the IIS (consistency, speed, perceived fairness) be improved?
   f. Should individual proof be introduced into the IIS?
   g. Should we be aiming to harmonise around the European list of diseases?
   h. Should we be seeking higher levels of benefit?
   i. Should IIS benefits be offset against means-tested benefits?
4. Civil and state compensation
   a. Is the balance between the two mechanisms right?
   b. What about interaction between civil and state systems
      i. offsetting of damages against benefits?
      ii. protection of damages in assessing means-tested benefits?
      iii. Should we be moving towards a single system?
      iv. How can we link compensation and prevention?
5. Rehabilitation
   a. What should the balance be between employers, insurers, state (DfEE), voluntary sector and NHS provision?
   b. Can rehabilitation ever work in small firms, and if not, what next for sick or injured workers in small firms?
   c. Should workers ill or injured by work have a specified higher level of job security (as many workers assume they have)?
   d. Can rehabilitation work in the long term?

e. What happens when mismatches between jobs available and workers' potential accumulate over the years?

f. What should be the balance between prevention and rehabilitation?

6. Research

a. Any ideas for advancing the poor standing of occupational health research in the UK?

b. Should there be a legal right of access to workforces for HSE researchers?

c. Are we looking for bipartite or tripartite commissioning of research?

d. Should there be a separate fund for labour initiated research?

e. Should there be bursaries to fund advanced training in state of the art institutes elsewhere?

Appendix two

The health and safety project team

Chair of Project Team: Professor John Hendy QC *Old Square Chambers*
Research leaders: Professor Phil James and Dr Dave Walters
Project coordinator: Carolyn Jones *Director, IER*

Members of Specialist Working Groups and Consultants

Dr R M Agius *Senior Lecturer in Occupational & Environmental Health, University of Edinburgh*
Becky Allen *Occupational Health Review, IRS*
Richard Arthur *Solicitor, Thompsons*
Simon Auerbach *Solicitor, Pattinson & Brewer*
Professor Mathias Beck *Professor of Risk Management, Glasgow Caledonian University*
Professor Brian Bercusson *Professor of European Law, University of Manchester*
David Bergman *Centre for Corporate Accountability*
Damien Brown *Barrister, Old Square Chambers*
Nigel Bryson *Health Safety & Environment Officer, GMB*
Professor Noreen Burrows *University of Glasgow*
Phil Carpenter *Negotiations Officer, IPMS*
Stephen Cavalier *Solicitor, Thompsons*
Louise Christian *Partner, Christian Fishers Solicitors*
Alan Dalton *Board Member of the Environment Agency*
Martin Day *Partner, Leigh Day & Co Solicitors*
Pamela Dix *Disaster Action*
Dave Feickert *TUC European Office*
Howard Fidderman *Editor Eurosafety, IRS*
Dr Tony Fletcher *Public Health Policy, London School of Hygiene*
Michael Ford *Barrister, Doughty Street Chambers*
Rosina Harris *Lewisham College*
Tom Jones *Solicitor, Thompsons*
Matt Kelly *Barrister, Old Square Chambers*

Peter Kirby

Peter McNestry *General Secretary, NACODS*

Richard Meeran *Solicitor, Leigh Day & Co*

Tony Myhill *ISTC*

Theo Nichols *University of Bristol*

Andrea Oates *Health & Safety Officer, Labour Research Department*

Rory O'Neill *Editor Hazards and Workers Health International Newsletter*

Roslyn Perkins *Health and Safety Advisor, BBC*

Graham Petersen *South Thames College Industrial Relations Unit, London Hazards Centre*

Simon Pickvance *Senior Research Fellow at De Montfort University Centre for Occupational and Environmental Health Policy; Occupational Health Adviser, SOHP; co-editor Workers Health International Newsletter*

Doug Russell *Health & Safety Officer, USDAW*

Marc Sapir *Director, European Trade Union Technical Bureau for Health & Safety*

Margaret Sharkey *Research Officer, UCATT*

Gary Slapper *Open University*

Roger Spiller *National Secretary, Health & Safety, MSF*

Steve Tombs *Criminal Justice Group, Liverpool University*

Stephanie Trotter *President Co-Gas Safety and Vice President of Consumer Safety International*

Laurent Vogel *Research Officer, European Trade Union Technical Bureau for Health & Safety*

Ian Walker *President, Association of Personal Injury Lawyers*

Professor Andrew Watterson *Centre for Occupational & Environmental Health, De Montfort University*

Celia Wells *Cardiff Law School*

Charles Woolfson *Faculty of Social Sciences, University of Glasgow*